The Complete Handbook of Pruning

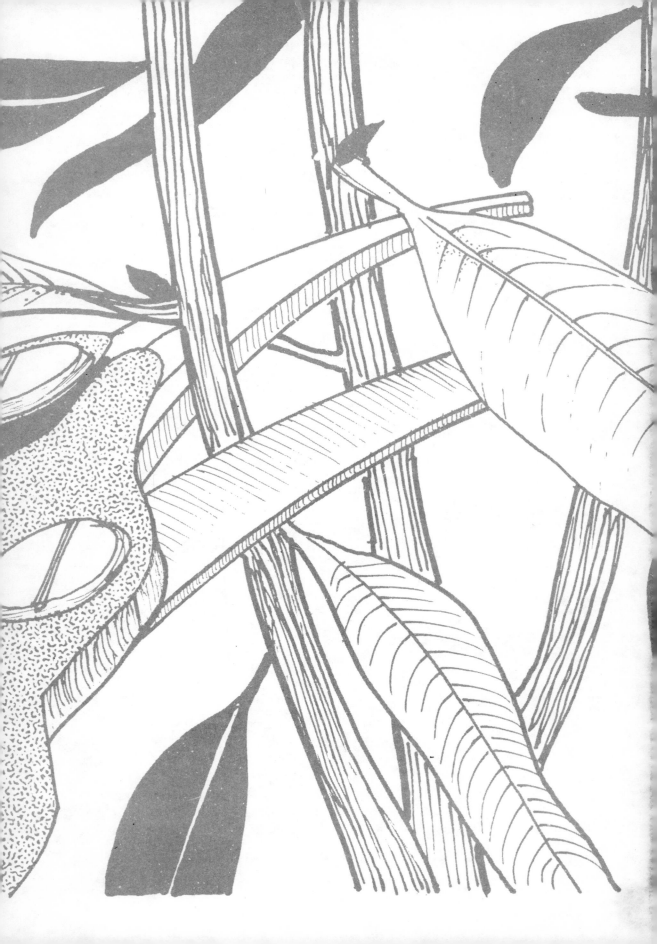

The Complete Handbook of Pruning

Edited by Roger Grounds

with contributions by

Brian Halliwell
Assistant Curator, Royal Botanic Gardens, Kew

and John Turpin NDH

Macmillan Publishing Co., Inc.
New York

Macmillan Publishing Co., Inc.
866 Third Avenue, New York, N.Y. 10022
Collier Macmillan Canada, Ltd.

Printed in the United States of America

Contents

1 Introduction

To prune or not to prune? This is a question that always seems to face gardeners. Most feel they ought, but are not sure why or how. It is accepted practice for the orchard, fairly frequently carried out in the rose garden, but rather haphazard elsewhere. Most often it is only performed when a shrub or tree begins to encroach on its neighbor, a path or a building.

Pruning is often looked upon as the answer to make a barren tree fruitful. Carried out correctly, it will—eventually! Years of neglect cannot be rectified in one season. The unknowing pruner who cuts because he thinks he ought but does not know how, often finishes up with no flowers at all through too hard pruning or carrying out the operation at the wrong time of year.

Some gardeners are obsessed by tidiness and formality, wanting their trees and shrubs to be like smart soldiers on parade. Trees are lopped to a standard height, while for shrubs out come the clippers and branches and twigs are cut back to a predetermined size and shape all identical. As spring advances, the gardener becomes distraught for he has not allowed for the different angles or rates of growth that now reduce his parade-ground effect to a shambles. Strict uniformity is in any case acceptable only in the parterre which is laid out in symmetrical geometric designs where lines have to be kept sharp.

What then is pruning? Why does one prune? When? How?

Pruning can be described as the removal of a part or parts of a woody plant by man for specific purpose. The reasons for pruning are:

1 To train the plant
2 To maintain plant health
3 To obtain a balance between growth and flowering
4 To improve the quality of flowers, fruit, foliage or stems
5 To restrict growth

Training

A woody plant will flower or bear fruit earlier if it is allowed to grow naturally. Pruning delays flowering but in the early years it ensures a framework of strong well-spaced branches, later to produce flowers and fruit. A tree of desired size and shape can be fashioned which is not only well balanced and delightful to the eye but carries flowers or fruits where they can be easily seen and reached. Building up of the initial framework makes for easier management of tree, shrub or climber in later years.

Maintenance of plant health

A beautiful tree is a healthy one! Control of pests and diseases is essential and it is easiest if the cause of these afflictions can be removed as early as possible. Pruning is one way in which this can be done. In early years, pests and diseases interfere with training; in an aged specimen they hasten the end; while at all stages of growth they are unsightly, can destroy flowers or fruit and weaken branches—the fall of a large branch can mean severe damage or death to the tree.

Routine spraying can control pests and some diseases in shrubs and young trees but it becomes impracticable if not impossible on large trees, when pruning is the only feasible method of control. Most diseases that attack trees enter through wounds and spread via the conducting tissue, killing off branches as they extend their hold. If disease reaches the trunk death usually results. The disease organism travels beyond the wood it has killed off and its presence in apparently healthy wood can be detected by a brown interior staining. When diseased wood is being removed always cut back to sound wood, that is, wood where there is no staining.

Dead wood is always unsightly and likely to break off, causing damage. It is the breeding ground for disease (eg coral spot, Nectria cinnabarina) which can spread from the dead wood to the live. When removing any wood include also that which is dead.

Maintaining a balance between growth and flowering

A tree or shrub in strong active growth produces few flowers and in fact too heavy pruning can delay or even prevent flowering. Pruning in the early years should be sufficient only for training.

Once a tree has come into full flowering, shoot production will decline until at maturity very little annual growth is being added. In a mature plant it is the young wood which produces leaves and in many plants even the flowers, while with age the quality of these and the rate at which they are produced declines. It is therefore desirable to encourage a woody plant to maintain the production of young wood by judicious pruning.

Improvement of quality of flowers, fruit, foliage and stems

The more flowers and fruit a plant produces, the smaller they become, as can be witnessed on an unpruned rosebush or fruit tree. Pruning reduces the amount of wood and so diverts energy into the production of larger, though fewer, flowers and/or fruit. The length of flower spikes on an unpruned butterfly bush *Buddleia davidii* may be 4 in. but can exceed 12 in. on one that has been hard pruned.

Leaves are produced only on current season's growth. The more vigorous this is the larger will be the leaves, and in plants with colored leaves the more intense will be the coloring. Shrubs grown for their foliage, summer or autumn, variegated, colored or dissected, are pruned hard annually.

Some deciduous shrubs have colored barks which are especially delightful in winter. The best color is produced on young stems and the greatest length and most intense color results from hard pruning.

Restriction of growth

Trees and shrubs left to develop naturally grow bigger and bigger, becoming an embarrassment where space is restricted, and so pruning becomes necessary to keep them within bounds.

Other forms of pruning

There are some jobs carried out in a garden which are also forms of pruning although they are not always recognised as such. The cutting of flowers from woody plants for home decoration is a type of pruning. Trimming of hedges is restrictive pruning applied to a row of shrubs. Topiary, the clipping of bushes to bizarre shapes, is a combination of training and restrictive pruning, and so is pleaching, used to make living screens or arches. Tree surgery is an extreme form of pruning to maintain a tree in a healthy condition.

For the gardener pruning is essentially an artificial operation and he may well question its necessity when it does not occur in nature. But it does! Some shrubs and trees not only shed leaves annually but they also shed twigs, as in *Tamarix* and dawn redwood *Metasequoia glyptostroboides*. Eucalyptus saplings produce a thicket of shoots from which the strongest grow away at the expense of the remainder to become the leaders; the rest die. Later a long, clean trunk is produced by the natural shedding of branches.

Weather conditions such as wind, drought and frost (and, of course, fire) can remove portions of plants, usually the growing points; this affects development and the trees become shrub-like. Animals, as distinct from man, feed on young growth and often remove these succulent growing points so that trees fail to develop a single stem but produce many, thus remaining as shrubs. In Africa the opposite process is common: herbivores turn large shrubs into trees by feeding on young growth of the side branches and leaving the woody and unpalatable main stems untouched, so producing an arborescent effect. Pests and diseases too, just like animals, play a part in the natural pruning process and affect development of plants, again usually by destroying the growing points.

THE PRUNING OF ORNAMENTAL PLANTS

1
Training by Pruning

Most trees and shrubs grown in a garden are purchased from a nursery. It is useful for the reader to know how these were raised for it does have some bearing on pruning.

Woody plants may be on their own roots, having been raised from seed, cuttings or layers; or they may have a root system (rootstock) of one plant and the aerial part (scion) of another as a result of grafting (budding is only one form of grafting). Grafting is used to propagate trees and shrubs because:

1 It is the most reliable or only method of increase
2 By use of a selected rootstock it is possible to regulate the ultimate size of tree, eg as in fruit trees
3 It is possible to produce artificial types of trees, eg shrubs can be made into trees or pendulous shrubs can become weeping standards
4 It can induce earlier flowering, eg grafted tree magnolias flower earlier than those raised from seed

Trees may be grafted low, with their union close to the ground, or they may be high grafted onto stems of varying lengths. When planting, those that are grafted low should have their union buried unless the rootstock governs the ultimate size of the tree, as with flowering crabs on apple rootstocks; these are planted with their union well above ground-level.

Remember that grafted trees and shrubs are always likely to produce suckers from their rootstocks, and these, if left, grow away at the expense of the scion variety. Suckers should be removed as soon as they appear. Do not cut off at ground-level because all buds below will start into growth and where there was one sucker there will now be several. Scrape away the soil until the point of origin is exposed, then with a sharp downward pull remove the sucker;

this takes away the basal buds which cutting would have left.

Rooted cuttings, layers and graded seedlings are lined out in nursery rows and grown on for a year, by which time some of the shrubs may be ready for selling. The rest of the shrubs and the trees are grown on until they are big enough for sale.

DECIDUOUS TREES

These may be sold as whips which have a single straight stem and perhaps a few *feathers*, which are short side branches an inch or two in length. Whips are relatively cheap even if they are small, but they do allow maximum scope for training. They are sold bare-rooted and should be planted in the garden to the same depth as in the nursery; planting can be done during open weather at any time in the fall or spring. Staking may be necessary.

In the nursery or in your garden, these whips put on extension growth from the apical bud with development of feathers or side branches along the length of the main stem. These can all be retained for they help to thicken the main stem even if they slow down apical development. If all are removed, there is a greater increase in length of the leader but the main stem remains thin. An intermediate process known as feathering is often adopted. All side branches or feathers on the lowest third of the tree are removed; on the second third all side branches are reduced to two or three buds, while the top third is left unpruned except to remove any upright branch which is challenging the leader. This practice continues annually until there is a sufficient length of trunk, and then the branching system is allowed to develop. Such pruning is usually done in late autumn.

Trees are trained in two main ways; as standards which have a clear 6-ft. stem from the top

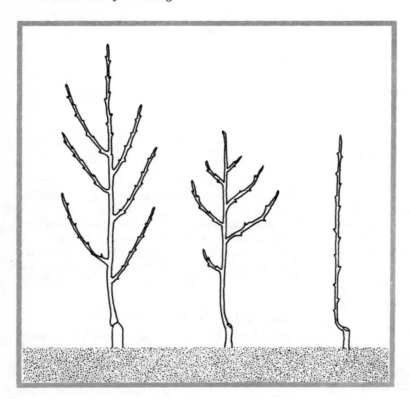

Types of fruit trees as usually purchased. *Left* a maiden, *center* a feathered maiden, and *right* a 2 year whip growth

of which the framework is allowed to develop; and as central leaders where the leader is continuous, with branches arising all the way along the length of trunk.

Standards

When the young leader reaches about 7 ft. 6 in. the tip is removed to encourage branching. Again, this operation is usually carried out in late autumn. This produces a tree with a clear 6-ft. trunk (a half-standard has a clear 3-ft.-6-in. stem). Standards are the form commonly offered for sale by nurseries and are well suited to small-growing trees such as crab apples and mountain ash. But for the larger-growing trees the central leader should be used.

Central leaders

Instead of being stopped, the leader is allowed to grow unchecked, and in the nursery branches are allowed to develop at 6 ft. from the ground. When the gardener is training, a clear stem of 8 ft. is preferable to allow mowing beneath in

comfort; if he has purchased the tree from the nursery with a clear stem of only 6 ft. this can easily be rectified. The length of clear stem to aim for depends, of course, on the kind of tree and the general habit of growth. In a number of trees branches become partly pendulous with age and sweep downwards; such trees are better with a trunk of 15 ft. or even more to keep branches clear of the ground. When branches are allowed to develop, they should be spaced at intervals along the length of the trunk. At the same time aim to produce a well-balanced head by allowing branches to develop only at planned points around the circumference.

Maidens

Grafted trees in their first year grow away very strongly, making anything up to 9 ft. of growth. These are usually clear stems, though they may also have feathers, and are called *maidens*, being sometimes sold as such. They are trained in exactly the same way as has been described for standards and central leaders.

Feathering: one of the methods of training a young tree into a standard. Above: the first year's training. Below: the same tree one year later

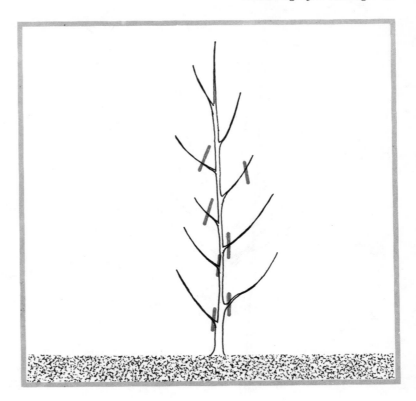

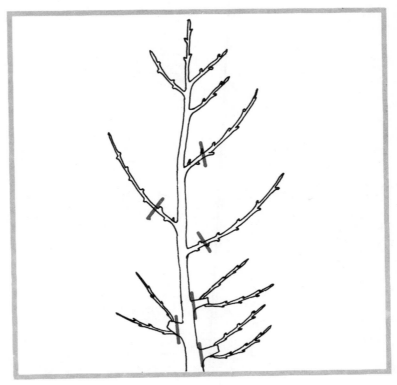

A double leader. When a tree throws two leading shoots like this one or the other must be removed

Pruning of different types of standard trees. The tree on the left has its leading shoot pinched out, and will produce a branching head; the tree on the right is left with its leading shoot and will develop into a more or less pyramidal tree

Pendulous trees

A few of these, eg weeping willows, can be raised from cuttings. A single leader is selected, feathered and supported, and sold by the nursery in varying lengths of stem. On planting in the garden, secure the main stem to a long stout pole, 12 ft. high if possible, and train the leader up this, feathering annually. When the top of the pole is reached, the main framework can be trained in.

Pendulous forms of normally upright trees— eg beech, ash, elm—are grafted. They may be grafted low which is to be preferred when the leader is tied to a stake and feathered. Most often they are high-grafted onto stems of 6 ft. and upwards. When planted in the garden, the leader should be cut back to where it is bending over, and all other branches reduced. Select the strongest shoot and train upwards, securing to a 12-ft. stake. When the top has been reached a framework can be trained in, and after the crown has attained sufficient proportion the natural weeping habit can be allowed. This will produce a graceful tree with plenty of height for the hanging branches. When pendulous branches are allowed to form on top of a 6-ft. or 8-ft. stem the result is squat and ugly.

In some forms of pendulous tree the leader continues its upward development without the necessity of being tied to a support.

EVERGREEN TREES

In the nursery evergreens are allowed to develop with a central leader but all side shoots are retained. Sold as either container-grown or balled, they should be planted in the garden, in a position protected from wind, and staked. Planting is best carried out in spring. Retain the central leader and the side branches as long as possible, although some trimmings of these, and some thinning where crowded, is beneficial, and this, again, should be done in spring. As with deciduous trees, the main branches are not allowed to form under a height of 8 ft. from the ground, and crowded and crossing branches are removed and so are double leaders. If trees have attractive barks, as in some species of *Arbutus,* the leader should be feathered so as to expose the trunk as soon as possible.

Conifers

These are allowed to grow naturally in the nursery, apart from the removal of surplus leaders, until they reach the size at which they will be sold. When planted in the garden, the single leader should be retained, any leader competition being removed in spring, and also any branches low down on the tree which begin to grow away strongly. Most conifers should be allowed to retain their side branches as long as possible; they should not be removed until they die naturally. An exception might be made with those trees which have a naturally pendulous habit.

Do not allow the main framework to develop too low down on the tree. The first main branch should not be allowed below 8 ft. from ground-level. Conifers with pendulous branches should not be allowed to develop their main branches under 12 ft., so that they will sweep down towards the ground gracefully. Conifers such as the *Chamaecyparis* cultivars may develop several leaders, which in their early years may be unnoticed and cause no trouble for they grow vertically and close together so that the desired shape is maintained. But as the trees age the trunks begin to fall outwards under the weight of their side branches and so spoil the outline. To correct this condition the trunks must be tied together. This need not happen if one keeps only a single leader, although with certain fastigiate forms such as the Irish yew (*Taxus baccata* 'fastigiata') several leaders have to be trained, and tying in of these at a later date is necessary.

Some conifers remain shrub-like, eg *Cephalotaxus* and some of the forms of yew (*Taxus*), and these have several leaders. They can be allowed to develop naturally, being occasionally trimmed to shape or to restrict growth. Dwarf or small-growing conifers, too, are left to develop naturally even if they have a multiplicity of leaders.

It is important that conifers having a tiered habit, eg pines, firs, and spruces, should retain only a single leader. Leaders can be damaged by animals, pests, or the weather, but should this happen a group of new leaders will develop of which the straightest and strongest only should be retained.

TRAINING SHRUBS
Deciduous specimens

Sold most often in nurseries as bare-rooted, these should be soaked in water prior to firm planting to the same depth as in the nur-

A sequence showing the pruning of a young standard ornamental tree. The purpose of this pruning is to keep the center of the tree open, and to prevent it from developing a double leader

sery. Grafted specimens should be planted with their union just below ground-level. Following planting, select and retain three or five of the strongest shoots, cutting back side shoots to two or three buds and reducing their length by about half. This should encourage new shoots to develop near to ground-level in the following growing season; in the next winter these stems are cut back again to half of their new growth. At the same time the center of the bush is opened up by removing crossing branches and any clutter of short shoots. Cut back the remaining side shoots to two or three buds and thin where crowded so as to produce a well-balanced, evenly spaced framework.

Evergreens

Sold either as balled specimens or as container-grown, these are planted in spring to the same depth as they were in the nursery, having first been given a good soaking. Select the three

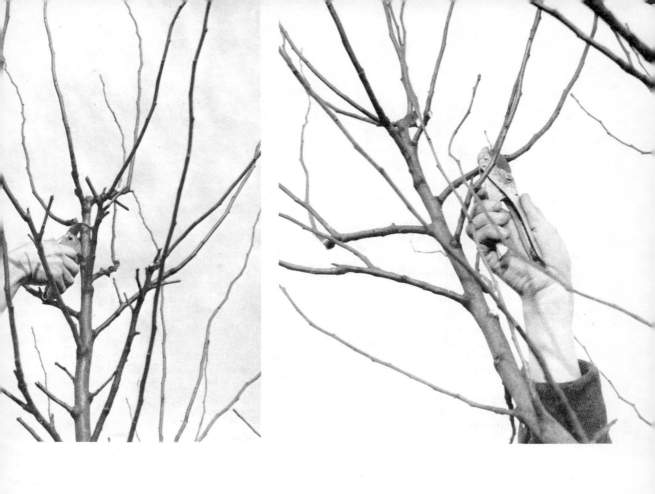

strongest shoots, reducing the remainder, and lightly tip or remove their growing points. In the following spring, thin out crowded branches and open up the center of the bush.

Tender shrubs

Most often sold in containers, they are best planted in spring after the danger of frost has passed. Ensure that plants from containers are not root-bound otherwise they will be slow to establish and will rarely anchor well, always being liable to blow out of the ground, especially when they produce large tops. Deciduous subjects should have their shoots reduced by half and their side shoots cut back to two or three buds. In the following spring repeat the process, thinning out and opening up the center of the bush. Evergreens should be lightly tipped or have the growing point removed after planting. In the following spring, thin and open up the center of the bush.

2
Pruning of Established Trees and Shrubs

As an annual operation and prior to any kind of pruning a number of basic tasks must be performed. All dead, damaged and diseased wood, and suckers at their point of origin, must be removed from grafted plants. Crossing branches and thin crowded shoots should be cut out, and thin weak shoots removed completely or cut hard back. Shoots which are showing reversion, a common complaint with the foliage of variegated plants and an occasional occurrence with flower color, eg in camellias, should have the offending branch traced back to its point of origin and removed. All these tasks should be carried out in the spring.

PROCEDURE FOR ESTABLISHED TREES

Once a tree has received its initial training pruning becomes negligible, although any strong branch which develops from low down on the tree, or any other that is growing near to the vertical, should be removed. Autumn is the best time to do this. The central leader will decrease in vigor over the years until it ceases to be a leader, while the crown will become more rounded or flattened. At all times the aim should be to maintain the outline of the crown and any branch that spoils this should be reduced or removed. Ensure that main branches are spaced evenly along the length of the trunk without too many developing from one small area. Periodical shortening of limbs may be advisable to reduce the possibilities of damage in gales, but problems of large dangerous limbs, bracing, propping or tree felling should be referred to a qualified tree surgeon (*see also* page 135).

Trees growing in restricted areas need regular attention to prevent encroachment. This should be carried out when they are fully dormant, offending branches being cut back to a point where a younger side branch originates.

Remove some of the oldest branches each year. Aim to continually train in young main branches so that old wood can be removed entirely. Do not in desperation hack the main branches back so that all that remains of the tree is the trunk with the bases of limbs! Too often one sees this kind of treatment meted out to street trees and nothing looks more hideous, especially in the winter months.

Some trees, eg lindens, develop twiggy growth along the length of their trunks, and this can spoil their appearance. These shoots should be removed regularly by rubbing them off while they are still soft or by cutting off carefully when they become woody. A chemical is now available which if sprayed or painted on the trunk will prevent or drastically reduce the appearance of such growths.

PRUNING OF ESTABLISHED SHRUBS

The method and timing of pruning deciduous shrubs is governed by the age of the wood on which flowering takes place: this may be on current season's growth, or on one-year-old wood or spurs. Evergreens and tender plants are considered separately, and so also is pruning carried out for a special effect.

Shrubs flowering on current season's growth

Growth has to be made before flowering can take place, so shrubs within this group tend to flower in summer and autumn. If left unpruned, shrubs grow higher but with reduced vigor, more flowers are produced but these are smaller and poorer in quality. Hard pruning means the removal of a large amount of wood so that the energy of the bush is diverted to fewer shoots and flowers which are consequently larger and of better quality.

Pruning is carried out when bushes are dormant. Weather permitting, February and

The pruning of shrubs which
flower on the current season's
growth. The object is to remove
those shoots which have
already flowered

March are the best months. All shoots are cut back hard to within two or three buds of ground-level or a framework.

Another method is to cut half the shoots back to two or three buds and the remainder to a half or third of their length. Hard pruning delays flowering but with this treatment the flowering period can be extended and the quality of flowers is still high. The following winter these longer shoots are removed completely; some thinning of resultant shoots is beneficial in May.

When shrubs of this nature flower in flushes or flower continuously, dead-heading should be practiced to improve their appearance and to prevent them expending energy on ripening fruit. This consists of the removal of the dead flower and if possible two or three buds on the flower stem; cutting is to be preferred, for though some stems can be easily broken off, others sustain damage to neighboring buds.

Strong growth and good quality flowers following hard pruning depend upon plentiful food supply, so apply a base dressing of a general fertilizer at the rate of 2–4 oz. per sq. yd., the heavier dressing for old and well-established shrubs.

Shrubs flowering on one-year-old wood

Growth is made in one growing season and in the following year flowers are produced either on this growth or on short laterals coming from it. This group tends to flower in the early part of the year from January until May. Individual shrubs can be pruned directly after flowering, or pruning can be delayed until July when all the shrubs in the garden falling within this group can be treated; if berries are to be a feature pruning takes place in March.

Shrubs in this group can be left unpruned but they tend to become too tall, encroach on their neighbors or create an unmanageable tangle of growth. Pruning then consists of removing the twigs which have flowered. If young growth is breaking, cut back to where there is a strong young shoot growing in the desired direction. Thin out the remainder of the shoots, especially opening up the center of the bush so as to improve air movement which

The pruning of shrubs which flower on one-year-old wood. The shoot which has flowered is removed, leaving the new growth to flower the following season

will help to ripen wood. Unripe wood is especially a problem during a wet season when growth is lush. In August of such a year, carry out a further thinning to help ripen wood. As less wood is removed in the pruning of this group smaller applications of a general fertilizer are required. This can be at the rate of 1–2 oz. per sq. yd. annually, or double the rate every second year.

Shrubs flowering on spurs

A spur can be described as a branch, usually a short one, which will produce its flower buds on one-year-old wood but will continue each year to produce more on the same branch; sometimes the wood has to be two years old before flower buds are produced but new flower buds continue to be added in subsequent years. These shrubs grow strongly in their early years, producing few flowers, but as growth slows down, so spurs begin to form naturally and there is a reduction of extension growth. When this stage is reached, pruning can almost cease.

Pruning may need to be practiced during the early years of development, especially if space is limited. Once a framework has been formed all annual stems are cut back to three or four buds, with the exception of the leading shoot on main branches. The following year some of these buds will grow away, and if the others do not flower they will form flower buds to produce blossom in the next year. Once these flower buds form, any growth which develops beyond them should be removed.

Evergreens

Their main attraction in the garden is their foliage in the winter months. Most evergreens are liable to damage if exposed to cold winds or subject to prolonged low temperatures when the ground stays frozen for long periods. This shows itself by death of branches or the discoloration and death of leaves. Pruning of evergreens is carried out in April just before growth commences. Cut out any winter-damaged wood, trimming back discolored foliage; thin and trim to shape. If evergreens are also grown for their flowers, they invariably produce these on one-year wood and so pruning is delayed until after flowering.

Tender plants

As these are always liable to damage by frost pruning is delayed until May when the danger of severe frost has passed. Those flowering on one-year-old wood are not pruned until after flowering. Pruning consists of the removal of winter damage, removal of stalks which have carried flowers and some thinning.

Pruning for special effects

Shrubs are not always grown in gardens for flowers and fruit; sometimes stems or bark or leaves have more appeal.

Shrubs such as the forms of Cornus or of Salix are planted for the effect of their colorful bark during the winter months. Bark color is most intense on young wood and the best effect is from the strong young shoots that result from hard pruning. *Cornus, Kerria* and *Rubus,* and others with a suckering habit, are cut down to ground-level in March. Those which do not have this habit are treated rather differently. Several leaders are permitted, each of which is feathered so as to expose the lower part of the stems at an early age.

Ailanthus altissima (tree of heaven) has large compound leaves which are attractive, but as it makes a tree 60 ft. in height this is obviously too large a subject for a small garden. The young plants, however, make a very strong growth in their early years and on these strong unbranched shoots are even larger leaves; this habit can be retained if shoots are cut down to ground-level annually in March and fed copiously.

Many shrubs have more attractive foliage, either summer or autumn, than flowers. Leaves are only produced on current season's growth and those of the largest size are on the strongest growth. Deciduous shrubs with variegated, colored or cut foliage are pruned hard almost to ground-level or to a framework during the winter months and fed copiously.

The pruning of hedges with shears. This is particularly useful on plants like laurel where any leaves that get cut brown at the base

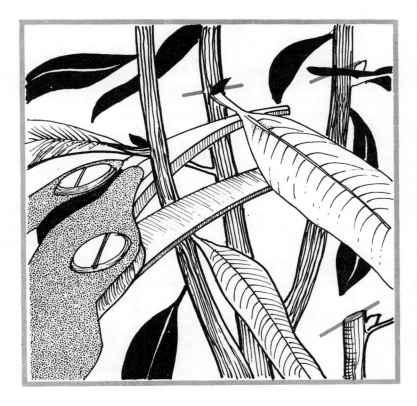

3
Climbers
and Wall Shrubs

Climbers are plants with weak stems that take themselves up towards the light by means of their climbing habit. Plants have adapted themselves to this habit in a number of different ways:

1 by twining stems, as in the common honeysuckle *Lonicera sempervirens,*
2 by twining leaf stalks, as in *Clematis* species,
3 by tendrils, as with the *Vitis* species,
4 by tendrils producing pads that stick to their supports, as in Boston ivy *Parthenocissus trocuspidata,*
5 by roots produced on aerial stems which stick to their support, the best example being English ivy *Hedera helix,*
6 by thorns which hook on to support, as in climbing roses.

In addition there are plants, lax of habit, that get themselves up to the light by flopping over rocks, trees or other shrubs.

In the garden climbers can be used for a number of purposes: for covering pergolas, walls and fences; for training up poles; and for growing over or through trees and shrubs. One chooses the climber most suitable for a particular site. On a bare wall or fence only a climber that sticks itself to its support can be used, but if the wall or fence is provided with a trellis or parallel wires almost any kind of climber can be grown.

SUPPORTS FOR CLIMBERS

Trellises should be securely fixed in position after having been painted or treated with wood preservative prior to erection. The thickness of timber to be used depends on the type of plant it has to support. Strong climbers such as wisteria produce heavy stems, so strong supports are necessary. Metal trellising can be used as long as it has been painted or galvanized and,

again, the heaviest gauge is necessary for the strongest climbers. If climbers are going to be grown against wooden buildings or fences that will need painting periodically, it is advisable to fix the trellises to their support with hinges so that they can be swung away at painting times.

Parallel wires are quite suitable and easier than trellising to install and maintain; they should be of a sufficiently heavy gauge to support the climbers and galvanized, painted or covered with plastic. Fix them to the wall horizontally, with 9–12 in. between them, through eyebolts with strainers at each end to keep the wires taut. Upright canes, vertical strings or wires are often added to give extra support.

Trees make admirable supports for strong-growing climbers. The trees should be mature, but even dead trees can be used; in fact if there is a dead or unsightly tree in the garden which cannot be removed, the best thing to do is to hide it behind a climber. Dead trees should have their smaller branches removed, and with live trees it is advisable to reduce the canopy to admit more light. After planting the climber insert a cane or fix vertical wires to take the stems up into the branches of the tree.

Pergolas again need strong climbers that get their stems up on top of the structure as quickly as possible. The reduced light from the top cover causes lower leaves to fall, resulting in bare stems near to ground-level, but selected climbers can be planted in to hide the bareness and introduce some color lower down.

Supporting poles may be of trimmed timber, cut tree branches or metal. Wooden poles need to be treated with wood preservative, at least at their bases, and metal posts must be painted or galvanized to prevent rusting. Grow the weaker climbers on poles, or be sure to prune each year so that there is never more growth than the poles can support.

When shrubs are to act as supports, choose

those that are well established, reasonably vigorous and of moderate size. Select climbers which are not themselves of vigorous growth and be prepared to be ruthless with them at pruning time so that the supporting shrub is not smothered.

PREPARATION OF SITE FOR CLIMBERS

At the foot of walls, fences and pergolas the soil is usually poor and often contains large amounts of builder's rubble, all of which should be removed. Near a house wall there may be drains or underground pipes and it is advisable to know their positions. Dig over the soil, incorporating as much organic matter as possible; thorough preparation is essential prior to planting to provide optimum conditions for growth. The soil at the base of walls, fences and pergolas receives little rain and remains relatively dry. Never plant your climber less than 9–12 in. away from a wall, and water new plantings until well established.

Soil at the base of trees and shrubs is also poor, so to ensure quick establishment take out a hole 12–18 in. deep, fill with fresh soil and organic matter and plant into this. Here, too, the soil is dry, with little rain reaching it naturally and the tree or shrub competing for what there is; so, again, water after planting until the climber is established.

PLANTING CLIMBERS

Climbers are now almost always container-grown and on sale throughout the year. April planting is the best, but planting can be done throughout much of the year as long as attention is paid to watering until the climber is established. After planting, reduce the stems to a half or even a third of their original lengths to encourage young growth to develop at or near to ground-level. Select three or five of the strongest shoots, provide them with canes, vertical wires or strings, and train them in the desired direction of the permanent support. At the end of the next growing season reduce all the leaders by about a half, cutting the weakest shoots even harder; thin out crowded shoots and space well the main stems. Repeat each year until the allotted space has been filled with a well-spaced framework.

Regular attention is necessary in the training of climbers, and when growth is in spate they need almost daily attention. Clematis and other plants that have twining leaf stalks, if neglected even for a week, produce an unmanageable tangle which defies the patience of Job to unravel. Moreover, if climbers that stick to their supports either by roots or sucker pads are allowed to wander in the wrong direction, it means that the shoots must be pulled off whatever surface they have fastened on and they will not stick again.

Evergreens are treated similarly to deciduous climbers but pruning is always less severe, the growth being tipped rather than cut hard back. Do ensure that the bases of walls and fences are adequately clothed to start with and keep them so.

ESTABLISHED PRUNING FOR CLIMBERS

The same rules apply to established pruning for climbers as for shrubs, that is the method and timing are dependent on the age of the wood on which flowers are produced. Those which flower on **current season's growth** can be cut hard back to an established framework during the winter. More often they are cut to ground-level and in this case all the training described in the earlier part of this chapter can be ignored. When pruned hard, flowering is delayed, but the flowering season may be extended by leaving in some shoots which are trimmed but not cut hard; these are removed completely in the following year. Very late flowering climbers in this group, or in areas where early frosts are prevalent, are cut much less severely, with growth being reduced by about half and this removed completely in the following winter.

Climbers flowering on **previous season's wood** are pruned after flowering. Shoots which have flowered are removed or cut back to where new growth is developing, and thinning out of remaining growth follows. Train in new shoots as they develop, keeping only enough to comfortably furnish; any surplus should be removed.

After a framework has been formed, the **spur producers** have all side shoots cut back to two or three buds during March. For some this treatment may have to be carried out twice, once in July when shoots are cut to four or five buds and again in March when any resulting growth is shortened back to two or three.

Climbers on poles need drastic pruning at all times, irrespective of the group to which

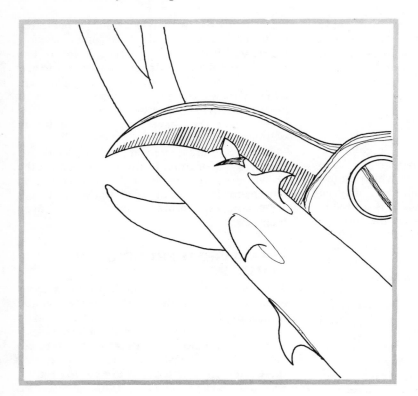

Parrot-beak shears in action

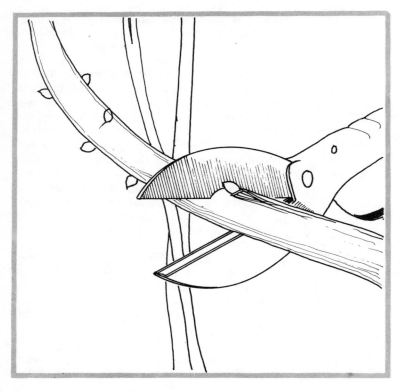

Anvil-type shears in action. The cut should be made with the blade on top of the bud so that the actual position of the cut can be seen

*Clematis jackmanii.
Considerable forethought
should be given to the pruning
of clematis since the species
and the different groups of
hybrids need pruning in
different ways*

they belong, to ensure that no more growth is permitted than the poles can support. **Climbers on trees,** on the other hand, need no further pruning once they are established, unless growth becomes excessive and threatens the tree or if a clutter of dead wood occurs. On pergolas pruning is minimal, just thinning out to prevent overcrowding and removing shoots which wave about in the wind and annoy people passing beneath. Some training in of young growth should be practiced so that periodically some of the oldest stems can be removed.

SITING AND PLANTING OF WALL SHRUBS

An area close to a wall is more protected than one in the open, and of course drier. In summer walls absorb as well as reflect heat and so, being warm, and dry, help to ripen wood.

A south wall is the warmest and driest and well suited to growing plants considered to be tender or needing to have their wood thoroughly ripened to flower freely. A west wall is almost as good. An east wall, however, is not suitable for early flowering shrubs; flowers of many plants can withstand some freezing without damage as long as they can thaw out slowly, but winter or early spring flowers are likely to be damaged in the early morning sunshine on an east wall. Such a wall is better suited for the growing of sprawling or climbing plants than for plants considered to be tender.

On a north wall there is no direct sun, and so it remains moister with less fluctuation of temperature, hence cooler than a more open position. A north wall, therefore, is well suited to shade lovers and shrubs requiring cool, moist growing conditions in summer.

When there are south or west walls in the garden it is possible to be more adventurous in the choice of plants and to try out trees or shrubs which are classed as tender in a particular district for growing in the open. Shrubs which, when grown in the open, flower sparsely or not at all, especially after a wet summer when wood fails to ripen properly, often flower profusely against a wall. West and south walls offer protection to shrubs that flower in winter months by allowing flowers to develop fully and remain open and undamaged by the cold.

Shrubs for planting against a wall may be offered bare-rooted, balled in the case of evergreens, but many, and especially the tender ones, are now sold in containers. Planting is best carried out just before growth starts, which will be April for some of the deciduous shrubs, but in most cases May planting is preferable. Plant firmly, 9–12 in. away from the wall, and finish up with a shallow depression in the soil around the main stem so as to facilitate watering, which should continue until the shrubs are well established—on each occasion giving a good soaking.

Training wall shrubs

Wall plants which are naturally trees can be trained to a single leader. A single-stemmed young plant should be chosen and headed back in April to about 9 in., above the lowest wire, or 2 ft. from the ground if on a trellis. Insert a strong stake or fix a vertical wire up which the leader is to be trained.

In the following growing season, the uppermost buds will develop. Select the strongest and train in as a new leader. Take the next two shoots and tie on either side of the leader to canes fixed in position at an angle of 45° to the vertical; any surplus shoots are stopped at four buds. In the following April, lower the branches to an angle of 60° (keeping the side branches at an angle allows extension growth to develop). Meanwhile the leader is beheaded at 9 in. above the next wire or about 18 in. above the first pair of branches when growing on a trellis. The strongest shoot is again tied in as the leader, and two more are tied in at 45° while surplus shoots are stopped at four buds. In the following April again, the bottom pair of branches is brought to the horizontal, the second tier dropped to 60°, surplus shoots stopped at four buds and the leader again beheaded.

This practice continues until the uppermost wire or the top of the trellis is reached, after which the leader can be allowed to grow on. In July or August of the following year, the leader is then removed just above the top tier.

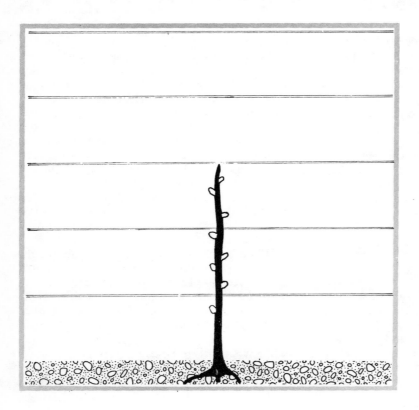

The training of climbers. The first illustration shows the plant in April of its 1st year after planting, showing where the shoots should be nicked. The 2nd illustration is a close-up showing precisely where the shoots need to be nicked. The purpose of nicking is to make the buds grow out more horizontally than they would otherwise. The next illustration shows the plant having made growth following nicking. The following picture (p. 26) shows the shoot being tied down to the supporting canes in April of the 2nd year, and the nicking of the buds on the new leader. The next illustration shows growth made during the 2nd growing season and the last illustration (p. 27) shows a tree being tied down and nicked again in April in the 3rd year after planting

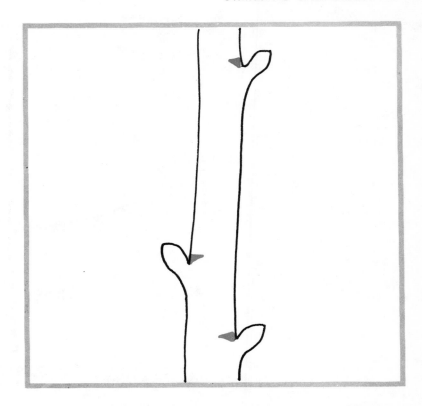

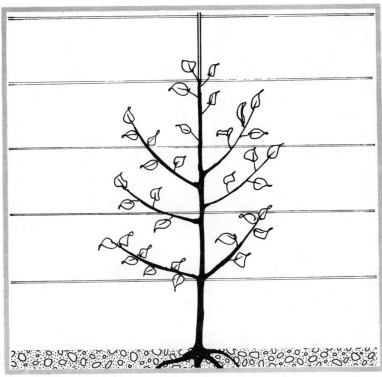

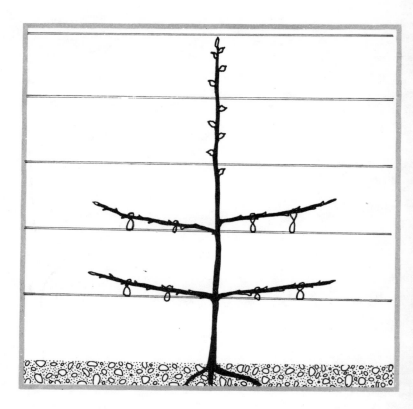

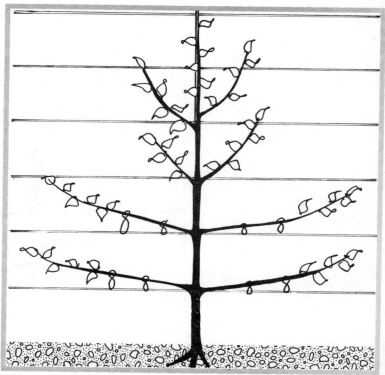

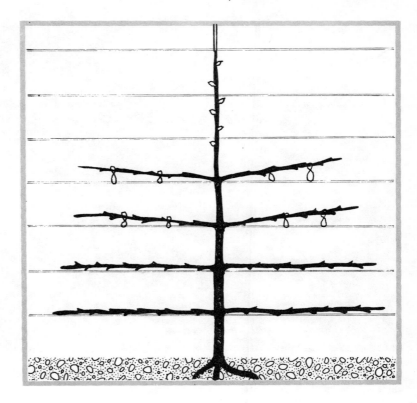

Once the bottom tier has been tied in horizontally, flowering can be allowed to take place. At all times any branches coming away from the wall are removed.

The above method may be slow but it builds up a well-balanced framework, provides good cover low down and flowering is progressive.

The following is a simpler method, best suited for deciduous subjects, and while not as good as the one just described it produces results more quickly and still provides reasonable cover. On a single-stemmed young plant, cut a notch just above the buds that you wish to form branches during April. This forces those buds into growth which is allowed to develop untied while the leader is tied to a central stake or wire. In the following April or May, the best-placed side branches are pulled down towards the wire and secured near the leader but not tied so tightly as to lie at the horizontal. Any surplus shoots are cut back to two or three buds. Notching again is carried out and the resulting shoots are allowed to grow freely while the leader is secured to its vertical support. In the next year, prior to growth starting, the lowest branches resulting from the first year's notching are pulled down and tied at the horizontal. Those resulting from the previous year's notching are again tied loosely. This continues up to the top of the wall when the treatment of the leader as already described (page 24) is repeated.

Another method of training a tree, which is also well suited to most shrubs, is to produce a fan-trained framework. Plant a single-stemmed young plant and make a cut 3 ft. from ground-level. Insert four stakes, the lower pair at 45° and the upper at about 30° from the vertical. When growth starts, select the strongest four shoots and train up the stakes, tying in at regular intervals. When planting a branched shrub select four stems and remove the remainder. Just prior to the commencement of the next growing season, cut back these four shoots to a third of their original length. Of the shoots produced, select two from each stem and tie to suitably fixed wires or strings, pinching back the remainder. At the end of the next growing

Wisteria chinensis is probably the most popular of all climbing plants. It needs a sunny position and regular pruning to obtain the best results

season there will probably be a sufficient framework built up for shrubs, after which established pruning can begin.

Trees will need another season to complete the framework. Prior to the commencement of growth, all the leaders are reduced to about half of the length of wood produced in the previous season. Of the resulting growth select only two shoots, pinching back the remainder. Space these out and tie into position; if there are too many shoots any that are crowded can be removed completely. Now that the framework is complete, established pruning can commence.

ESTABLISHED PRUNING OF WALL SHRUBS

Tender shrubs and trees, especially evergreens, are usually allowed to develop with the minimum of pruning. In May cut out any winter damage, thin out crowded shoots, remove old flower stalks and cut back any shoots coming away from the wall. The same rules apply to tender shrubs as to all others, except that pruning is usually carried out later, that is, in May when the danger of frost has passed.

Deciduous trees and shrubs flowering on current season's growth can be cut hard back to the framework although sometimes some young stems are left unpruned apart from a light tipping.

The pruning of **deciduous trees and shrubs flowering on previous year's growth** is delayed until after flowering, when that growth which has flowered is removed, cutting back where possible to where new growth is breaking. Of the new growth, select only enough shoots to comfortably fill the available space and remove the rest. Those which are **spur bearing** will have all young shoots shortened back to two or three buds until a spur system has built up.

Irrespective of the type of pruning, periodically train in some new shoots into the framework so as to be able occasionally to remove some of the oldest wood.

4
Roses

Roses are occasionally raised on their own roots but in the main are grafted. Those on their own roots include a few climbers, shrubs or species roses raised from cuttings, though most species are raised from seed; in all of these, shoots coming from below ground-level can be allowed to remain, for none will be suckers.

REMOVAL OF SUCKERS

Most roses offered for sale are grafted, having a root system different from the aerial part of the plant. These roses may produce suckers and the gardener must be on the alert to deal with

them. They usually arise from below ground-level, but this is not always the case with bushes that have been high planted so that the graft union is above soil-level. Equally, not all shoots rising from below ground-level need be suckers if bushes have been planted with their union below ground-level. Suckers on common bedding roses have smaller and more numerous leaflets than the rose variety, they are plain green, and either have no thorns or more numerous and smaller thorns. As there are several rootstocks in use for the commercial production of roses there is no one single type of sucker to watch for.

Rose bush as bought from nursery, showing the point of union of the graft, and the balance between top growth and root development

Bush rose prior to pruning. The illustration shows wood of different seasons' growth, thereby indicating how the shape of a rose is built up and retained

Whenever suckers are seen they should be removed; when they are small and young it is easier to do than when they are older and have become woody. Suckers should not be cut off at ground-level because this encourages subterranean buds to grow away and the result is several suckers in place of one. To deal with them effectually first scrape away the soil and expose their point of origin, then take the sucker in a gloved hand and pull sharply downwards; this removes both sucker and basal buds.

On standards (tree roses), rub off any shoots which develop along the main stem and remove those that arise from below ground-level.

On species roses that are grafted it can be very difficult to detect suckers for there is a wider range of rootstocks used in their propagation and the suckers from some of these are very similar to the scion variety and difficult to identify.

PLANTING OF ROSES

Container-grown roses mean that roses can be sold throughout the year. Although more expensive, they do allow the buyer to see just what he is buying, and planting can take place throughout much of the year, providing they are watered until established if in active growth.

The biggest demand, however, is still for bare-rooted roses which are offered for sale in the winter months. Planting of these can safely take place at any time from leaf-fall until early April. See that the union is set just below soil-level, or if the roses are on their own roots plant them to the same depth as they were in the nursery.

Standard or tree roses should be planted with a stake of sufficient strength to hold the rose tree firmly. Use a 4-ft. stake for half-standards, 6-ft. for full standards and 8-ft. for weeping standards. Wooden stakes should be painted or treated with a preservative and driven into the ground until the top is just below the graft union; secure twice, at about 9-in. above the ground and just below the union. Weeping standards should be provided with a framework over which to train their weeping stems.

A standard rose as bought from a nurseryman showing the point of union of the graft with the substantially greater root development usually found in standard roses as compared with bush roses

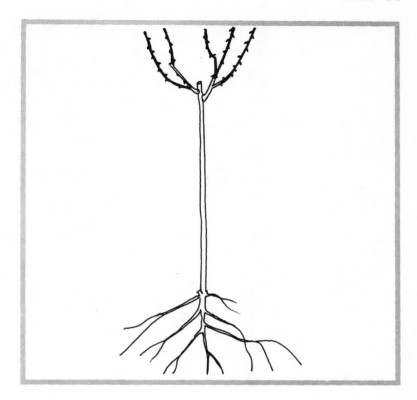

INITIAL PRUNING

Bedding roses planted late in the season are pruned at planting time. All roses can be pruned when planting but it is more usual with early plantings to allow them time to establish, pruning in March. All shoots are cut hard back: the weaker to two or three buds, the stronger to four or five.

Standard hybrid teas and floribundas are pruned less severely to seven or eight buds of the union.

Climbing hybrid teas and floribundas are reduced to about half their original length. Too hard pruning of this group can result in their reversion to the bush types of which they are but sports.

Wichuraiana climbers are cut to within 9 in. of the ground, and **weeping standards** to the same distance from the union.

Shrub and **species roses** are restricted to three main stems, the rest being removed completely. Those remaining are cut to about a third of their original length, all side shoots growing into the bush are removed and the rest cut to within two buds of the main stems.

PRUNING OF ESTABLISHED ROSES FLOWERING ON CURRENT SEASON'S GROWTH

Roses fall into two groups for pruning purposes: those flowering on current wood and those producing flowers on growth of the previous year. The main sections within the first group are: hybrid teas, floribundas, polyanthas, grandiflora, hybrid perpetuals, hybrid musks, miniatures, china roses and the *rugosa* forms.

Time of pruning

The timing of the pruning of this group flowering on current wood has long been controversial, every month from October to May having been recommended. Late March and early April is still the most popular period because it is claimed that shoots resulting are more likely to escape late frosts. But already at this time sap is rising and growth has begun, so some of the plant's energy will have been wasted, and in some varieties stems bleed following late pruning. Shoots which develop after this pruning are strong and succulent and therefore very susceptible to severe damage should there happen to be any late frosts. By May, disease organisms are active and likely to invade such damaged tissue.

Autumn pruning has now been generally discontinued. In a mild autumn pruning can force bushes into growth which is killed in the winter. Pruning when the bushes are dormant is undoubtedly the best time. If, following early pruning, buds do start into growth the shoots develop very slowly and are hardy, acclimatizing themselves as they grow, and so are better able to withstand damage from late frosts—although they can be damaged by earlier severe weather.

The gardener who has difficulty in making up his mind about when to prune should try bushes at different times and then decide for himself.

The tools required

A pair of shears is adequate for most of the wood, plus loppers for thick wood and a narrow-bladed saw for the thickest or for awkward spots where shears cannot be used. Strong leather gloves make the operation less painful.

It is most important to ensure that cutting blades on shears are sharp and correctly set, with anvils in good condition. Blunt or badly set shears result in tears and bruising which may be followed by die-back and/or disease infection.

Techniques and principles of pruning

Bedding roses can flower well and profusely if never pruned, but the framework becomes hard and woody and grows upward with each year. Eventually new growth diminishes, flowers are of poorer quality, the bush is cluttered with dead and dying wood, and disease becomes a problem. Light pruning has a somewhat similar result even if the upward development is slower

Newly planted H.T. rose, showing just how severely these should be pruned. Weak shoots should be pruned right back to buds and stronger shoots back to five buds. Very few people ever prune newly planted roses hard enough

Pruning a rose. A close-up showing precisely how and where pruning shears should be placed to obtain the correct cut in relation to a bud.

Removing a large limb from a mature tree. First a cut is made at some distance from the main stem, and the weight of the branch removed. If any tearing occurs it will not affect the final pruned surface. The stump of the branch is then removed flush with the main stem, and the cut surface pared with a pruning knife until it is smooth. Finally the wound is painted with a pruning compound, which prevents diseases entering the exposed wood and acts as a temporary bark until the tree's own bark grows across the wound.

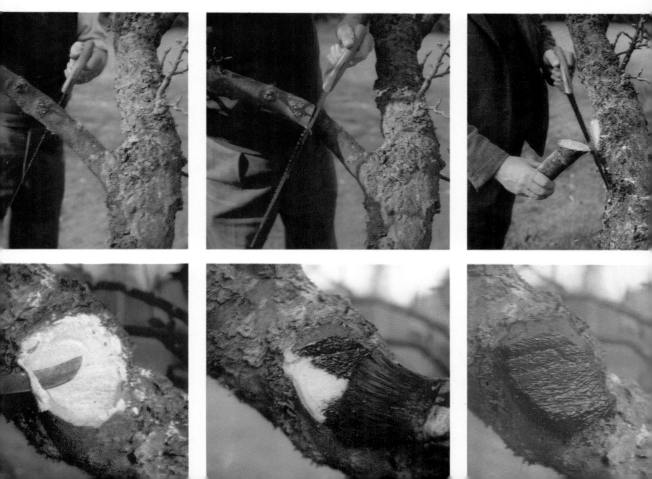

Pruning a bush rose prior to planting. The aim is to achieve a balance between top-growth and root growth. The plant in the first picture is completely out of balance, with far too much root in relation to its top-growth. In the final picture a balance has been achieved.

▲ Pruning a rambler rose. The first picture shows the unpruned rose at the end of a season's growth. It is then completely removed from its support, laid out on the ground, pruned, and then tied back into position.

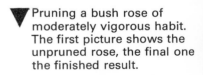

▼ Pruning a bush rose of moderately vigorous habit. The first picture shows the unpruned rose, the final one the finished result.

Pruning a standard rose. It is worth noting that in addition to shortening back the shoots, weak shoots should be removed altogether.

Rosa 'China Town' trained as a tie-down rose. The main shoots are bent over and secured to the framework of wires.

Using loppers to
remove shoots from
a rose that would be
too tough for
shears. More
shears are ruined
by attempting to
use them to cut
wood that is too
thick or too tough
for them than by
any other type of
misuse.

Pruning a peach. The sequence shows
the reduction in the number of shoots.
The final picture shows the end result,
a fine crop of peaches.

Pruning of a high grafted weeping rose to produce a longer trunk. The illustrations show the sequence in its 1st, 2nd, and 3rd year

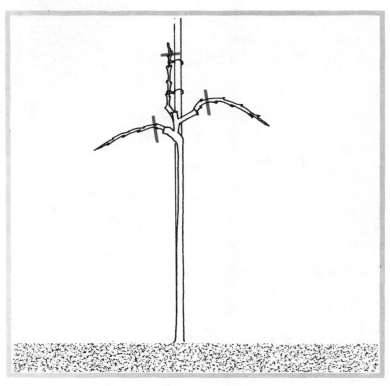

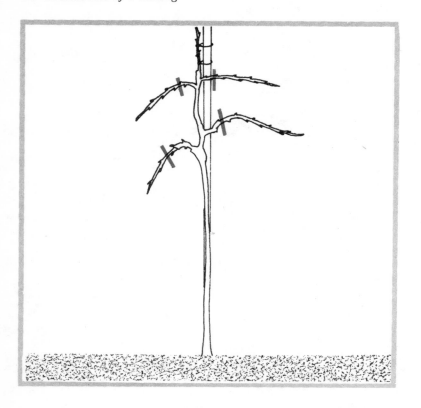

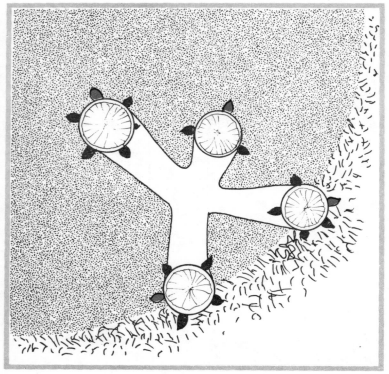

A plan view of a rose-bed showing a pruned rose as seen from above. The buds indicated in red are those which should be retained in order to produce a well-shaped plant

Incorrect pruning cuts. The picture shows on the left, the sort of cut made with a blunt instrument resulting in the tearing or crushing of the wood. The center illustration shows a cut made too high leaving a snag of wood that will die, probably becoming infected and which could therefore kill the whole plant. The drawing on the right shows a cut made too close to the bud: this will result in the wood dying back to the bud below and presents the same hazards as the cut made too high above the bud

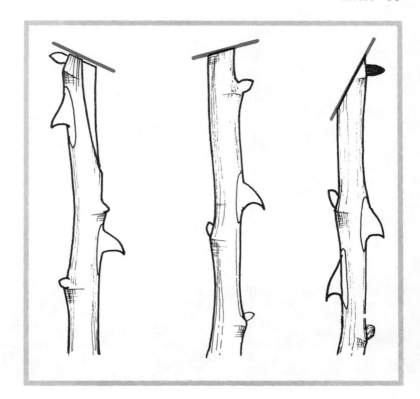

and there is no clutter, but flowers, though numerous, will be of poor quality. Hard pruning produces a small bush, well supplied with young growth on which flowers are few but of the best quality.

As with all pruning, one first carries out the essentials: cutting out all dead and damaged wood and any that shows signs of disease, thinning out crowded branches and removing shoots growing into the center of the bush. Look at the bush and observe the position, amount and ages of the wood. One-year-old wood is green, two-year-old is brownish-green and wood older than three years is brown or black. From old wood will emerge shoots of one-year, two-year and even older wood, and there will always be a preponderance of older wood at the base of the bush. The aim should be to have a large percentage of one-year-old wood in the bush with most of this coming from, or near, ground-level.

Each year cut out some old wood, removing it to a point where young wood is breaking lower down, or cutting out completely any

wood that has no younger wood, or very little, growing from it. At all times the aim should be to get rid of wood older than three years. On two-year-old wood, cut back to the lowest point at which young wood is developing, or if there is only terminal young growth, cut away about a third of the two-year wood. With one-year wood, cut back weak growth to two or three buds and reduce the strong to a half or a third of its original length. Strong-growing varieties should be pruned less severely than weaker ones.

When pruning, make the cut just above the bud horizontally or slightly sloping outwards. Cut always to an outward pointing bud. An exception is made on bushes growing on the outside of a bed when a shoot resulting from an outside bud would be damaged by the mower or perhaps tear the clothes of a passer-by. Stems in such a position can be cut so that the bud develops more or less parallel to the outer edge of the bed.

Small pruning cuts heal readily but larger ones on three-year-old wood need to be sealed.

The pruning of a newly planted rose bush. Very few people ever prune newly planted roses hard enough

Where a saw has been used, pare the cut surface with a knife before application. After winter pruning apply a spray combining both insecticide and fungicide to the bushes and the ground beneath.

Pruning removes wood in which food material is stored up and the plant has to make good the growth removed before it can flower. So whenever hard pruning is practiced it must go along with applications of organic matter or a dressing of a general rose fertilizer. Beds of roses which have been regularly pruned and fertilized can still be in good healthy condition, flowering well and producing blooms of good quality after sixty years.

Following the early spring pruning, bushes grow away and by June are producing their first flush of flowers. After these have faded, the bushes need to be dead-headed. This improves their appearance and diverts energy which would be used up in the production of fruits into the production of more flowers. Dead-heading does not consist of just removing the dead head but of cutting down to where new growth is emerging, or removing about one-third of the new growth. This is in effect a type of summer pruning which leads on to a good second flush and, if repeated, to a third in some years.

Treatment of neglected roses

After reading so far you may have decided that something ought to be done about those roses which have never been pruned! Can they be brought back into order? Yes, it is possible to get them into good shape again, provided that the bushes are not too old. It cannot, however, be done in one year; you cannot correct long-standing neglect overnight.

First remove all dead, damaged and diseased wood. Open up the center of the bush, cutting out crossing branches and thinning where

36

crowded; cut back all young wood to within two or three buds of their base. Feed well and apply a combined spray. This should stimulate the bushes into growth and some shoots should be produced low down on the bush.

In the following winter there must be more concentrated effort. Cut out all old wood arising above young shoots produced low down. Remove completely at least one old stem at, or as near as possible to, the ground. Reduce at least one of the older shoots by half and cut back hard all young shoots on the bush. Repeat the entire process the following year, cutting back all the time to where young growth is appearing low down on the bush. It will take at least three years to bring bushes back to normal but each year there should be an improvement in the amount of young wood produced and in the quality of flowers. If there is no response after two years, the bushes are too old and should be removed.

PRUNING OF ESTABLISHED ROSES FLOWERING ON ONE-YEAR-OLD WOOD

Included in this group are climbing hybrid teas and floribundas, wichuraiana climbers, weeping standards, most shrub roses and species. The best time for pruning these is immediately after flowering, but they are often left until the winter, especially when they have attractive fruits.

Climbing hybrid teas and floribundas produce new growth from ground-level which should be tipped and tied in. The strongest varieties do this reasonably freely and so all wood which has flowered can be removed completely. Unfortunately most kinds do not re-furnish readily and some, perhaps all, of their growth which has flowered has to be retained. Along these flowering canes, all the flowering laterals are cut hard back to two buds. The

The correct angle of pruning. The cut should always be made so that it slopes slightly back and away from the bud at which it is made

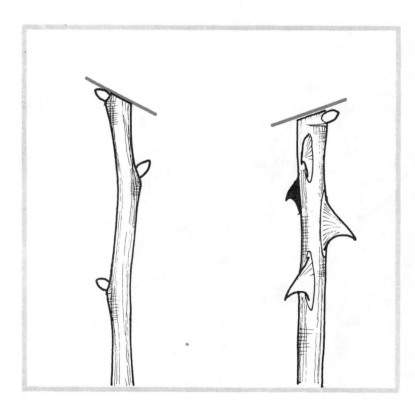

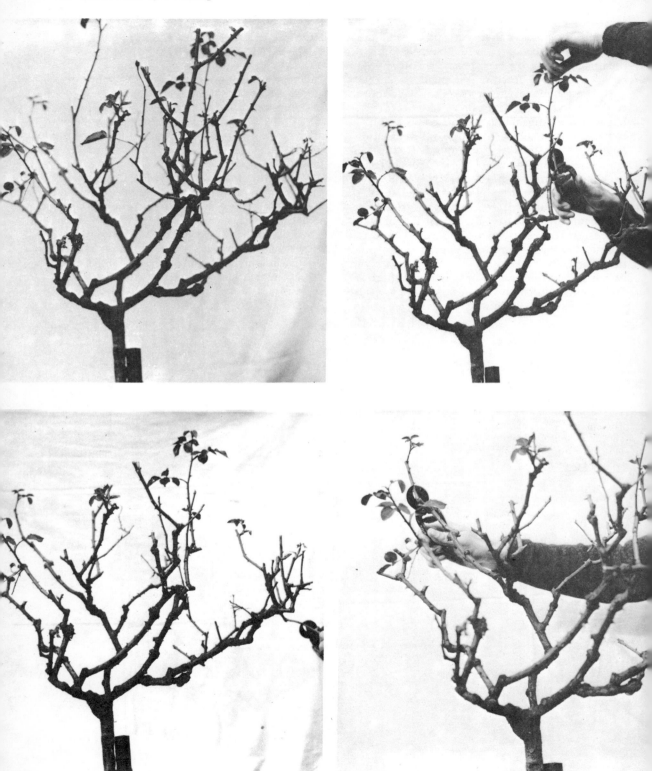

oldest shoots should always be removed whenever enough new shoots have been produced.

Wichuraiana climbers grow vigorously and produce an abundance of new shoots annually. All shoots, therefore, which have borne flowers are removed completely. In fact so strong are some varieties that far more stems are produced than are required. Whenever enough shoots have been selected and tied in so as to be well spaced, the remainder should be removed; do not be tempted to keep all just because they are strong and healthy. If these are growing over a tree, however, they can be allowed to grow unpruned except for the removal of dead wood. When climbing over a pergola, old stems are allowed to keep growing to provide a good covering, but all laterals which have flowered are cut hard back. **Weeping standards** are just wichuraiana climbers grafted on to a long stem. Following flowering, all stems which have borne flowers are removed completely.

Shrub and species roses can be left unpruned, but without attention they become thickets of tangled growth, their centers choked with blind, dead or diseased twigs. Annual pruning is desirable to open up the center of the bush and thin out crowded shoots. Tipping of young shoots in the winter months helps control mildew to which some kinds, eg *Rose × alba,* are particularly prone.

Roses with long arching branches can be shortened. Some species, eg *R. spinosissima,* have a suckering habit and should have the oldest and weakest stems removed completely. One or two are grown for the winter effect of their stems, eg *R. omiensis pteracantha* which has large red translucent thorns on its young stems. To encourage strong stems, all are cut to ground-level in March.

A few kinds are grown primarily for their foliage, either summer, eg *R. rubrifolia,* or autumn, eg *R. virginiana;* these can be cut hard back in March to increase the size of their leaves. If, however, flowers and fruit are also wanted, cut back half of the shoots hard and tip the remainder.

Rose species which are tender are grown against a wall for protection. *R. banksiae* flowers on sub-laterals of the older wood and sometimes on wood produced the previous year; after training in a well-spaced framework, it

Pruning a standard rose. A sequence showing the way in which a rose is gradually reduced in size by pruning in order to achieve the most effective growth for flowering the following season. It is very seldom a pruned rose is ever completely symmetrical

Climbing roses showing how the canes that have flowered should be cut out leaving the new canes. The example shown here is a Wichuraiana rose

Newly planted H.T. rose, showing just how severely these should be pruned. Weak shoots should be pruned right back to buds and stronger shoots back to five buds. Very few people ever prune newly planted roses hard enough

The pruning of shrub or species roses. The picture above shows the unpruned rose, indicating where the cuts should be made, and the picture below shows the rose pruned severely

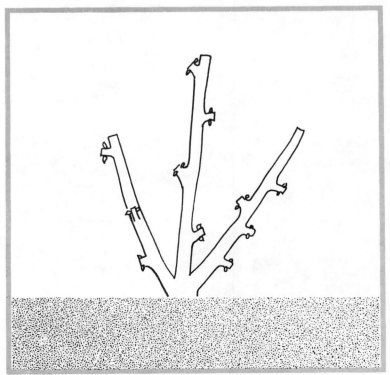

The pruning of a climbing rose. To be pruned properly, the whole rose needs to be taken away from the wall and laid out on the ground where the unwanted wood can be cut out. Only once this has been done should the healthy shoots from which the new flowering wood will sprout be tied back to the wall

does not need a great deal of pruning. Following flowering the surplus long shoots coming away from the wall are cut back, thinning takes place and the rest are tied in when some of the older wood is removed.

R. bracteata and its hybrid 'Mermaid' have pithy stems which are readily damaged by extreme cold, especially when wood fails to ripen properly after a wet summer. The young stems are very brittle and easily snapped off so care must be exercised when tying in. Carry out pruning in April, removing any winter-damaged wood, cutting back shoots which have flowered and thinning generally. When growing well, large amounts of shoots are produced and in a wet summer an end-of-August thinning of non-flowering shoots will aid the ripening of wood.

SPECIAL TYPES OF PRUNING

Hedges

Some of the more vigorous bushy kinds of roses can be used to make low hedges up to about 6 ft. in height. These are informal, producing flowers, and so are trimmed rather than clipped to strict formality. Among suitable floribundas are the old variety 'Frensham' or the newer 'Queen Elizabeth'; many shrub roses make good hedges, eg the hybrid musks and 'Nevada'; and of the many species suitable are *R. rugosa* and its hybrids and *R. rubiginosa* and its hybrid group, the 'Penzance Briars'.

Plant in well prepared ground at 3–4-ft. intervals and cut hard back to about 9 in. to produce strong growth from ground-level. In the following winter, remove about half of the new wood, and so on each year until the hedge has reached its maximum height. Hedges flowering on current season's growth are trimmed to shape in February and any dead wood removed. When flowers are from the previous year's growth trim after flowering.

Tie-down roses

This is a method of training strong-growing roses to induce maximum flowering. Some of

43

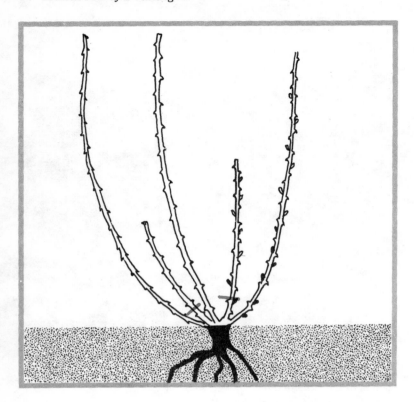

Tie-down roses. The training of tie-down roses, showing in the first picture a young plant being pruned in its second winter after planting in preparation for tying down to a metal frame (second picture) and the pruning of an established tie-down rose with the old flowering shoots being removed: the vigorous shoots on the left have to be tied down to flower the following season (third picture)

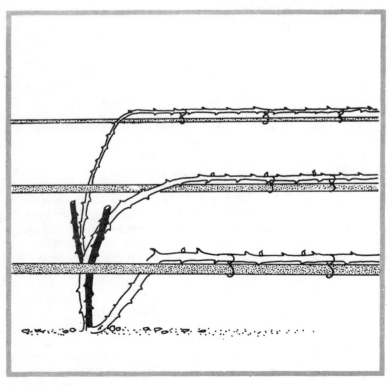

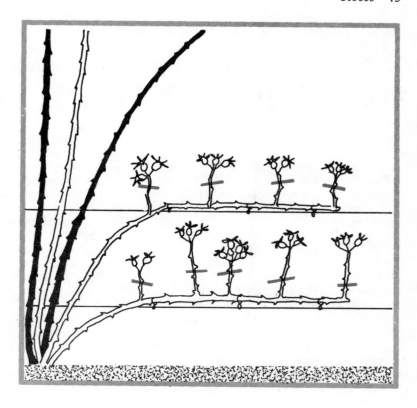

these strong growers produce up to 6 ft. of growth in one growing season with flowers on the ends of these long stems. During the last century, when hybrid perpetuals were the only roses which flowered more than once, their vigor was a problem and the tie-down system was devised to increase flowering. Today only a few of this group are grown, eg 'Hugh Dickson', but this method is well suited to such strong growers as 'Zephryn Drouhin', 'Frau Karl Drushki', 'Uncle Walter', some of the hybrid musks as well as 'Guinea' and 'High Noon'.

During the spring the sap, as we all know, rises to the highest part of the stem and the apical bud extends. When a bush is pruned, the top two or three buds develop and continue to extend, their ultimate length being governed by food material available and weather conditions. But if the shoot is tied down so that it is horizontal, all buds on the shoot are at the same height, so all develop equally. The tying down is done on a metal or wooden framework (appropriate to the size of the bed) which is fixed at 18 in. above ground-level. Its design is immaterial; it can be latticed, or of concentric circles or shaped like the spokes of a wheel.

Following a well-spaced planting, the stems are cut hard back to about five buds; weak shoots are cut even harder. In the following season several very strong shoots will develop. At pruning time these are tipped and tied to the framework so as to be horizontal, all of the stem remaining at one level. During the following summer short lateral growth will develop from each bud on the tied-down stem and produce flowers. In the winter months these laterals are cut back to two buds and any strong new growth is tied in. As the alloted space is filled, some of the oldest shoots can be removed each year.

Pruning should be carried out in March.

5
Tools
and Equipment

Tools used for pruning are numerous and varied and each has been devised for a specific purpose. There are three groups: knives, shears and saws (but *see also* Chapter 13 for hedge trimming tools).

KNIVES

Today the use of knives is limited because few people know how to use them properly, but in the hands of a skilled operator they are still the best pruning tool. There are a number on the market, of differing sizes and patterns, which are sold as pruning knives, but in fact almost any kind of knife can be used for pruning provided the blade is of good steel, capable of keeping a good edge, and is firmly set into the handle so that it cannot come loose under pressure.

A pruning knife must be sharp; a blunt knife is useless and can also be dangerous. More wounds are inflicted with blunt knives than with sharp ones, because more pressure has to be applied to make them cut and this is when they are likely to slip. When pruning, hold the branch below the point where the cut is to be made. Start with the knife behind the branch, just below the level of the chosen bud. With a slight upward movement make the cut at an angle, to finish just above the bud.

A knife should be sharpened on an oil-stone. Inspection of the blade will indicate how it was sharpened in the factory: often one side of the blade is flat and the other has been sharpened at an angle; sometimes both have been sharpened at an angle. Where possible, sharpen to the same angle as previously. However, some people find it difficult to keep a knife blade at a fixed angle, and they may have to compromise and sharpen both sides flat on the stone.

Keep your pruning knife for just this task. Don't use for cutting any old thing or for prying tacks out of wood or the edge of the blade will soon become chipped—even with constant care this can too easily happen. If the blade does become chipped, grind the edge down until it is again straight and then sharpen in the normal manner. Once a blade has been sharpened a keen edge can be produced and maintained as necessary by rubbing on a razor strop.

Though knives may not be in regular use for pruning there are some jobs for which they have to be used: paring smooth the bark after sawing off a branch; gouging out diseased material from a branch prior to painting with a wound protectant; trimming back young growth that has been damaged by late frosts; and removing twiggy growths along trunks so as not to leave basal buds. After use the blade should always be wiped clean and any matter adhering removed by emery paper. Rub the blade with an oily cloth and put a drop of oil on the pivot to make for easier movement.

PRUNING SHEARS

Shears carry out the work that was formerly done with the pruning knife. Their use requires little effort and no special skill; they are an indispensable aid to the gardener. There are two main types: the parrot-beak with two cutting blades, and the anvil with one.

Parrot-beak type

These are so called because of the shape of the cutting blades. They are available in several sizes, the products of different manufacturers varying slightly in design and size range. One type has a swivel handle which takes wrist fatigue out of the job. These are used in one hand and are capable of cutting stems of up to half an inch easily and up to three-quarters of an inch with care. Do not try to cut heavier wood with them. When cutting use a straight action and avoid twisting the blades.

After use, remove ingrained dirt with emery paper and before putting away wipe all parts with an oily cloth and put a spot of oil on the hinge and spring. When not actually working

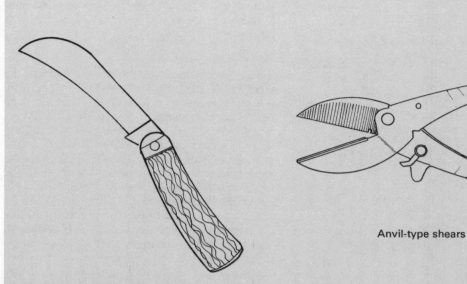

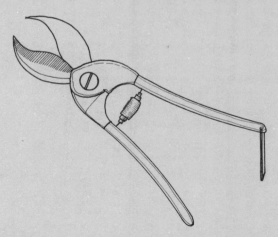

Anvil-type shears

A pruning knife. There is a definite art to using these knives and any competent rose nurseryman will demonstrate it to you. If you can master the art it will give a good, clean cut

Long handled pruners, also known as stumpers or loppers. The extra length of the handles gives one considerable cutting power, and these are designed to be used to cut hard, old wood

Parrot-beak shears

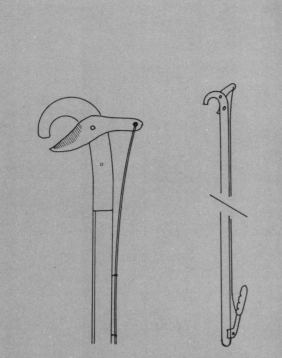

Long arm pruners. These are useful for removing relatively large branches from plants that would be too high to reach

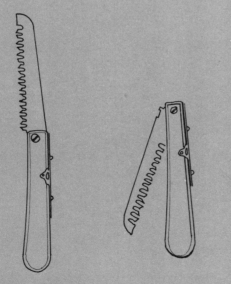

Narrow-bladed pruning saw. These folding types are particularly useful

with them keep the catch on and the blades together. Some manufacturers or their agents will service their shears for a small fee, and if these are in regular use annual attention is desirable.

Anvil type

These shears have an anvil which holds the stem while the single blade does the cutting. They are available in several sizes and with one or two special modifications, eg for cutting wire. They need a little more attention in handling than the previous type. Make the blade do the cutting; do not try to make the anvil push the stem against the cutting edge. Always have the blade where it can be seen and place the blade above the bud when making the cut. Again, do not attempt to cut wood that is too thick; like the parrot-beak type, these will easily cope with wood up to half an inch, and with care up to three-quarters. Avoid twisting the shears when cutting as this strains them and causes the blade to cut off center, which results in bruising or tearing of the bark. The blade must be sharp at all times and the anvil in good condition. After continued use the blade can cause a groove along the anvil or ingrained dirt may accumulate to provide an uneven surface and inefficient cutting with bruising and tearing will certainly follow. Sending your shears away annually for service ensures that they remain in good condition.

When a pruning job is finished see that all ingrained dirt, either on the blade or the anvil, is removed with emery paper and all metal parts are rubbed with an oily cloth. A drop of oil should be introduced into the pivot. Fasten when not in use so that the blade is kept against the anvil.

Long-handled shears or loppers

These are modifications of the anvil or parrot-beak type on handles about 18 in. long. The blade or blades open wider, and as with the longer handles there is more leverage the loppers can cope easily with wood up to three-quarters of an inch and with care up to one inch; their longer handles give a greater reach. Two hands are needed to operate them.

Long-arms or long-armed pruners

These are anvil-type shears fixed on the end of a pole which comes in varying lengths up to 9 ft. The single cutting blade is operated by a wire attached to a handle. When the handle is in the up position the blade is open; to operate, pull down the handle and this drives the blade on to its anvil. This high-reaching tool also needs two hands, one to hold and one to operate.

SAWS

Joiners' or carpenters' saws can be used for pruning, but saws manufactured for the job are to be preferred for they stand up better to the rougher work and are easier to insert and use in difficult places. Saws take over from shears and loppers when branches of more than one-inch thickness have to be cut.

Narrow-bladed saw

This type has one cutting edge, is between half an inch and an inch in width, and has a folding handle. It can deal with wood up to one and a half inches in diameter but above this the work becomes tiring. Its main use is to saw awkwardly placed small branches or to remove one branch where several are growing close together and loppers cannot be used.

Pruning saw

This is two-edged, with larger teeth on one side than on the other. It is used for branches up to perhaps 3 in. in diameter, the initial rougher work being carried out with the larger teeth and the final finishing cut made with the smaller. The one trouble with this type of saw is that it is unsuitable for dealing with branches growing close together, as damage can be caused by the second cutting edge. After use, remove sawdust from the teeth with a wire brush and wipe with an oily rag. Send away regularly for sharpening.

Grecian saw

The curved blade has teeth along one side only. It can be used for the same tasks as the pruning saw and is preferable to it.

Bow saw

Here we have a metal frame with a detachable saw blade which is capable of dealing with all branches as long as there is enough space to operate; replace with a new blade when the old one shows signs of wear.

When sawing off a small branch, take its weight so that it does not break away and tear the bark. If one does not have a free hand or

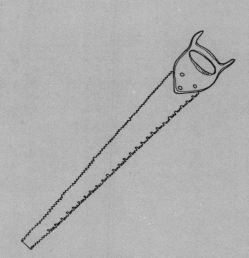

Pruning saw. Note that the teeth on one side of the blade are much coarser than the teeth on the other side. It is thus a dual purpose weapon

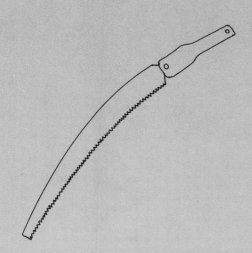

Grecian saw. This is useful for cutting old wood in confined spaces

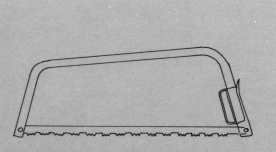

Bow saw. This is normally used for removing large branches

Platform stepladder, which is essential to the pruning of taller plants

if the branch is large, it should first be under-cut until the wood begins to pinch; then remove the saw and start on the top of the branch. Don't worry about being directly above the lower cut. This does not matter. As the branch parts from the tree it will break cleanly between the two cuts. The stub remaining should then be cut off neatly, finishing just slightly proud of the trunk.

A large limb should be removed in pieces. When in the center of the tree or high in the crown, large branches or parts to be cut away should be roped to higher branches so they do not fall and damage wood below (*see also* pages 137–139).

LADDERS AND STEPLADDERS

When pruning has to be carried out on trees and even on some large shrubs, some if not all of the branches may be out of reach and a ladder or stepladder will be necessary.

Stepladders should be in good condition and securely placed. When working on soft soil stand the legs on wooden planks. Household stepladders can be used but are not very comfortable for prolonged use. Aluminum platform steps are best, being light and durable with a relatively large area from which to work.

Ladders for tree work again should be in good condition and firmly placed both at the top and the bottom. Never work on a path without having someone below to hold the ladder, and in windy weather, tie the top securely before beginning. A safety belt gives a feeling of security and leaves both hands free. Try to work above the branch you are removing as this is less tiring than having to reach upwards and saw from beneath. And when dropping branches have a care for persons or property underneath. You may be legally responsible for any injury done. Finally, after having removed the wood, clear up, burn the twiggy growth and saw up the stout branches into lengths.

SEALING APPLICATIONS

The removal of any part of a plant causes a wound which has to heal. Just below the bark of a shrub or tree is a single, continuous layer of cells known as the cambium. Following a cut, these cells begin to divide, producing callus tissue which forms in a ring around the circumference of the cut and continues to increase inwards for varying distances, depending on

Removal of a large branch. The first cut is made on the underside of the branch, the second above, and the last nearest the trunk. The point of making three cuts instead of one is that if the branch tears away it does so at a little distance from the main stem and one can then cut back cleanly to the trunk

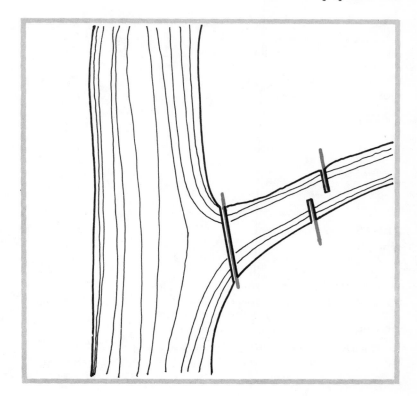

the size of cut, age, vigor, condition and kind of tree or shrub. On small young branches, the entire end of the cut may be sealed in this way, but on thicker and older wood healing may not be complete and callus may only form around the edge of the cut.

Roughly cut, broken, torn or bruised wood is slow to heal because the ring of cambium has been broken and a complete seal is rarely possible. Broken branches or those roughly cut with a large toothed saw should have the stubs taken off with a finer toothed saw and the edge of the bark pared smooth with a sharp knife. Where tears have taken place, all the edges of exposed bark should be pared smooth.

The importance of sealing

Fungus diseases are spread by spores which float about in the air. They can enter a plant through a wound and as soon as they take hold they multiply rapidly. There are two types of disease: parasitic, infecting living tissue, and saprophytic, invading dead tissue.

Parasitic diseases such as silver leaf spread throughout the plant along the conducting tissue, causing death of the branches as they proceed. They will always have advanced beyond the wood where external symptoms appear, and to cut back to healthy tissue all wood showing interior brown staining has to be removed. Saprophytic diseases attack the central part or heart wood of the tree, which consists of dead tissue—only the outer sheath is living. The spread of these diseases can cause cavities, and if continuous can invade the trunk, so weakening the tree. Some saprophytic diseases can also become parasitic; coral spot is one such disease.

The formation of callus tissue prevents the entry of disease organisms and so it is important that this healing process should be as rapid as possible. It is quite fast on young shoots but it can take a long time where old and large branches have been removed. All cuts above an inch should be treated with a wound dressing which provides a protection against disease entry until the healing process is complete. There are a number of brands available.

For those trees that are slow to heal, especially in the winter months (eg magnolias), pruning may be more suitably done in the late summer when callus tissue forms more quickly.

6
Pruning Control of Pests and Diseases

PESTS
Aphids
PLANTS ATTACKED Very many.

SYMPTOMS Colonies under leaves or on growing points. Distortion of leaves and growing points followed by early defoliation or death of growing point. Aphids spread virus diseases.

CONTROL Cut out badly infested shoots and burn; spray with malathion or lindane.

Leaf miners
PLANTS ATTACKED Various members of compositae and *Ilex* species and cultivars.

SYMPTOMS Tunnels or blotches within the leaves, at first white but becoming brown as the leaf ages.

CONTROL In light attacks spray with malathion: this should kill the pest though the damage will remain; in bad attacks cut away unsightly growth. When attacks are frequent, spray annually with lindane as the young growth begins to develop.

Stem borers
PLANTS ATTACKED Various, ·particularly pines.

SYMPTOMS Dying of young shoots, often the leader.

CONTROL Cut out and burn infested shoots.

Woolly aphis
PLANTS ATTACKED Apples, ornamental crab apples.

SYMPTOMS Colonies of pests surrounded by a cotton-wool-like mass. In bad attacks swollen, gall-like growth appears on branches.

CONTROL During pruning cut out infested shoots; spray with malathion.

DISEASES
Black spot
PLANTS ATTACKED Roses.

SYMPTOMS Black blotches on leaves.

CONTROL Gather up and burn fallen leaves and prunings; spray with captan or benomyl.

Brown rot
PLANTS ATTACKED Apples and pears, both edible and ornamental.

SYMPTOMS Brown soft rot of fruit on which appear gray or buff-colored pustules; during the winter the infected mummified fruits remain hanging on the trees. Spores can spread from these and infect buds of spurs and twigs, resulting in die-back.

CONTROL Remove all mummified fruit and burn; spray with captan.

Bud blast
PLANTS ATTACKED Rhododendrons, particularly garden hybrids.

SYMPTOMS Dead flower buds covered with dark gray fungal growths.

CONTROL Hand-pick and burn infected buds. This disease is spread by the rhododendron leaf hopper and these pests should be controlled by spraying, following flowering, with lindane or malathion to which is added zineb to control disease spores.

Canker

PLANTS ATTACKED   Various, particularly apples and pears, ornamental as well as edible.

SYMPTOMS   Dead areas on branches with raised, gnarled edges surrounding dead, papery, often peeling bark.

CONTROL   Most common on old trees or those in poor condition—a disease of neglect. Cut out branches where infections occur and burn. Where this is not possible, gouge out infected material with a sharp knife or chisel; paint all cuts with a wound protectant.

Coral spot

PLANTS ATTACKED   Various, particularly *Acer*.

SYMPTOMS   Orange pustules on infected wood.

CONTROL   This disease attacks dead wood from which it may spread to living, especially when this is in poor health. In some plants it will spread from dead wood to healthy material causing die-back of branches and in bad attacks the entire tree may die. Cut out all dead and diseased wood and burn; seal all cut surfaces. In bad attacks or with susceptible plants such as *Acer*, spray with zineb.

Die-back/grey mould botrytis

PLANTS ATTACKED   Various, but particularly roses.

SYMPTOMS   In winter it can be recognized on dead twigs by a water-stained appearance of the bark. In summer the die-back is accompanied by grey mould.

CONTROL   Cut out infected material and burn; follow by spraying with captan.

Dutch elm

PLANTS ATTACKED   All kinds of elm.

SYMPTOMS   The disease is spread by the elm beetle whose galleries can be seen under the bark on infected branches. Dead wood in crown of tree; early yellowing and defoliation of infected branches.

CONTROL   Where infection is light, cut out and burn diseased wood; in severe cases, fell and burn.

Fireblight

PLANTS ATTACKED   Most genera in the Rosaceae, the following being particularly susceptible, *Cotoneaster, Crataegus, Pyracantha, Pyrus* and *Sorbus*.

SYMPTOMS   Dead twigs with blackened dead leaves still hanging, looking as though burnt; seen in June and July.

CONTROL   Cut out and burn infected shoots. After each cut, dip cutting implement in methylated spirit to prevent spreading disease agent; seal all wounds.

Poplar canker

PLANTS ATTACKED   Most poplar species.

SYMPTOMS   Long narrow patches with sunken bark and gumming.

CONTROL   If the disease is extensive, no control is possible; fell and burn. In light infections cut out or gouge out infected wood back to healthy wood and seal all wounds; sterilize all cutting implements.

Powdery mildew

PLANTS ATTACKED   Many.

SYMPTOMS   White mildew on young leaves and stem.

CONTROL   Cut out and burn infected shoot tips; spray with karathane after pruning and at intervals of 7–10 days during the summer.

Silver leaf

PLANTS ATTACKED   Various, but particularly peaches, cherries, apples and plums, both eating and ornamental.

SYMPTOMS   Leaves take on a silvery or leaden appearance and die-back follows.

CONTROL   Prior to mid-July cut all infected material back to healthy wood; seal all cuts. Burn infected material.

7
Alphabetical List of Genera

Abbreviations

D	Deciduous	T	Tree
E	Evergreen	C	Conifer
L	Leafless	Cl	Climber
S	Shrub		

ABELIA DS Most species are tender and need a sheltered position or wall. In late April, remove winter damage, thin crowded shoots and remove some old wood.

ABELIOPHYLLUM DS A shrub with a sprawling habit, usually grown against a wall to give protection to its early flowers.

After flowering, cut out shoots on which flowers have been produced. If grown as a free-standing shrub, rather harder pruning is necessary following flowering to correct the sprawling habit.

ABIES (fir) EC Select a single leader and retain all side branches.

Abutilon, showing where pruning cuts should be made

54

ABUTILON DS All species are tender and usually grown as wall shrubs. In spring cut out winter damage and thin out crowded shoots. *Abutilon vitifolium* should be treated as a free-standing shrub and succeeds best where there is some summer humidity; the only pruning needed is dead-heading.

ACACIA ES/T All species are tender and require the protection of a south wall. Ensure that the base of the wall is well clothed and kept covered right throughout training; as most species are trees in their natural form growth is upwards and flowers too often are out of sight. Established pruning consists of dead-heading, thinning and the removal of dead wood in spring or early summer.

ACER (maple) DS/T A large family of varying habits, size and attractions all of which have to be considered when pruning.

Trees are trained to a central leader which is feathered. If the leader is lost a new one must be trained in or the opposite buds will result in two leaders; in some species it is difficult to retain a leader. Carry out pruning when fully dormant: some species bleed if cut when the sap is rising. Bushes may be allowed to have several leaders though often a central one is trained in but with all side shoots retained.

Colored leaf forms of *A. negundo* should never be pruned hard otherwise the resulting shoots revert to green. Training in the early days should consist of little more than pinching. Those trees grown for their bark should, through feathering, have their trunks exposed as soon as possible; an annual trimming of the previous year's growth on the striped bark maples will result in long colorful young stems. All species are likely to suffer damage from the fungus known as coral spot. This initially infects dead wood but spreads to the living, killing stems and even branches; if it girdles a young tree death can result.

ACTINIDIA DCl Slightly tender, vigorous twiners that need plenty of space. Once a well-spaced framework has been achieved by training in several long stems opposite and parallel, young stems are cut back in April to within two or three buds of this framework; repeat the process in July so as to build up a spur system.

AESCULUS (horse chestnut) DS/T Often these trees are slow growing in their early years. Select a leader and feather; retrain a new leader if the original is lost, or two will result because of opposite buds. There is a tendency to produce strong shoots low down on the tree and these should be removed, preferably during the winter months. With age the lower branches droop and touch the ground, so in training do not allow the lowest branches to develop under 12 ft. *A. parviflora* does not form a tree but clumps of vertical stems. Occasionally cut out the oldest of these and restrict spread if the clumps become invasive. This work should be done during the winter.

AILANTHUS (tree of heaven) DT Makes very strong growth when young: 9 ft. in one year is not unknown. Shoots are pithy and subject to winter damage, especially if not properly ripened. Keep to a single leader, retraining if the original is lost.

The strong young shoots with their very large compound leaves are sometimes used to give sub-tropical effects in gardens. To achieve this, cut all shoots back to ground-level in spring, just as the buds begin to swell, and feed copiously. Take care not to damage the root system; otherwise extensive suckering will result.

AKEBIA DCl Strong climbers which need plenty of space and which will become an unmanageable tangle unless regular pruning is practiced. In June cut out all shoots which have flowered and thin drastically any remaining. If pruning has been neglected, shear off at about 3 ft. from the ground, retrain a framework and start again.

ALNUS (alder) DS/T Plants for damp soils, grown especially for their winter catkins. Often they are allowed to develop without special training except for thinning out crowded branches. If a tree is required, select a central leader and feather. Colored leaf forms should be moderately hard pruned after flowering.

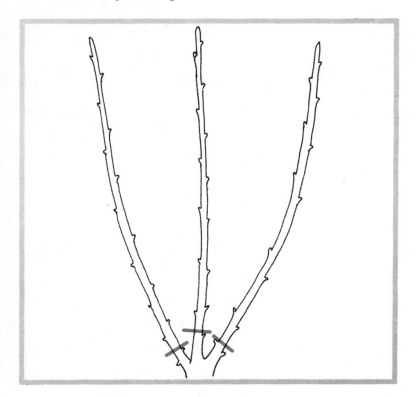

Coppicing or hard pruning, to achieve a sub-tropical foliage effect. This type of pruning is only suitable for one or two trees such as *Ailanthus altissima* or *Paulownia tomentosa*. The latter, when treated this way and grown in rich soil, will produce huge heart-shaped leaves up to 3 ft. across

AMELANCHIER (serviceberry) DS/T For pruning purposes, there are two types: one suckers and remains a shrub, the other becomes tree-like. The first is pruned in January when the oldest stems are removed; for the second, a central leader is trained, all side shoots being reduced but retained as long as possible.

AMPELOPSIS DCl All are strong growers and need plenty of space. They are well suited for growing through a tree where no pruning is required. If space is restricted train in a number of rods (mature shoots) and in January cut back all young shoots to within two or three buds of the rods. Bleeding will follow if pruning is delayed until the sap begins to rise.

ARALIA DS Stems arising from a rootstock are stout and pithy and liable to be damaged in winter if they do not ripen properly. The chief attraction is the large compound leaves of which there are variegated forms. Retain only a few stems and remove the rest at ground-level each spring.

ARAUCARIA (the monkey puzzle) DC Hardy in the United States through Zone 7. It makes a large tree and needs plenty of space. Select a central leader and retain all side branches until they die naturally.

ARBUTUS ES/T Some species are tender. Shrubs require little attention except to thin growths in April. Trees should have a central leader with all side shoots reduced but retained as long as possible. *A. menziesii*, *andrachne* and × *andrachnoides* have attractive barks; trunks can be exposed early by feathering.

ARCTOSTAPHYLLOS ES/T Some species are tender. Prostrate forms may need thinning; otherwise stems will grow over each other, shutting out light and causing the leaves to die off. The tree forms are usually trained to three or more leaders which are feathered during April to expose their colorful trunks.

ARISTOLOCHIA Dcl *A. durior* is hardy into coastal Maine, while other species are grown in the South and West. These are vigorous growers requiring plenty of space. After flowering drastically thin 'out shoots and reduce those that are wandering.

ARONIA (chokeberry) DS If grown for flowers and fruit as well as autumn color, thin out only the crowded branches during winter. If grown only for autumn color, reduce all shoots by half.

ARTEMISIA ES A few species are woody and these are somewhat tender. Remove winter damage in May and trim to shape. As these plants are grown for their foliage, flower spikes can be removed as they form.

ATRIPLEX ES Some species are tender. All kinds tend to sprawl, especially if grown in shade or a rich soil. Trim moderately hard in April to correct this habit.

AUCUBA ES Trim to shape in April occasionally cutting out some of the oldest wood. This shrub will respond to hard pruning if it becomes too large.

AZALEA *see* **Rhododendron**

AZARA ES/T All species are tender and, except in the mildest parts of the country, need the protection of a wall where they are fan trained. *A. microphylla* (Zone 8) is the hardiest species and can make a free-standing shrub or even a small tree in favored districts. After flowering remove shoots which have carried flowers, clear winter damage and carry out some thinning.

BAMBOOS ES (The different genera are all included under this heading for their pruning is identical.) Cut out discolored stems, dead and thin stems, as well as those which have flowered in April. The bamboos which spread by underground runner can be invasive and some means of confining them may be necessary. Once flowering begins death follows, not always immediately but each year thereafter the clumps decline.

BERBERIS D/ES Some evergreen kinds are tender and need shelter. All evergreen berries should be pruned after flowering, but if berries are wanted, delay until the following April when those shoots having borne fruit are removed. Most deciduous kinds form dense thickets and these should be thinned in July, removing completely at ground-level. If old bushes become unmanageable they can be cut down to ground-level after flowering.

BETULA (birch) DT Most birches have attractive barks even though these do not develop until the trees are several years old. Select a central leader and feather, exposing the trunk eventually to about 10 ft. before allowing branches to form. The leader in birches is frequently lost, and as leader competition is common reduce multiple leaders.

One or two species such as *B. populifolia* naturally develop several trunks, which can be an interesting feature in a landscape. To produce several trunks in a birch, cut the sapling back at planting time to about 3 ft., select the strongest shoots and train each as a separate leader.

Weeping birches should have a central leader trained to a support until there is a clear stem of 12 ft.

BUDDLEIA D/ES Many species are tender and need a south or west wall for protection; these are trained fan-wise, ensuring that the lowest part of the wall is kept clothed.

Buddleias which flower on current season's growth, eg *B. davidii*, are cut hard back to a framework in the winter; tender species are similarly treated in April. Buddleias which flower on the previous year's growth, eg *B. globosa*, are pruned following flowering when the shoots which have carried flowers are removed.

Buddleia alternifolia is best treated as a standard. Select the strongest shoots, removing the others, and tie to a stake; continue feathering until there is a clear stem of at least 4 ft., after which natural development can be allowed.

BUXUS ES/T If of tree form, select a single leader, removing competition; side shoots are reduced but retained as long as possible except if too crowded. The bush kinds, of which there are many different forms, should be trimmed to shape in April when some corrective pruning may be necessary, especially if heavy snow has caused any damage.

CALLICARPA DS All species are tender to some degree. Prune in April cutting out any winter damage and thinning out crowded shoots.

CALLISTEMON ES Profuse in California and Florida but tender elsewhere, needing the protection of a south wall. Growth is continuous, flowers being produced just behind the growing point. Seed capsules can remain on the shrub for years but, if left, these gradually reduce the rate of growth producing a gaunt, rather untidy bush. Prune then after flowering, removing the spent flowers and trim to shape.

CALLUNA (heather) ES Trim over the clumps in March, removing old flowers and most of last year's growth. The dwarf forms such as 'Foxii' and 'Foxii Nana' are not pruned at all except to remove dead wood. Plants grown just for foliage are often best trimmed as the flower spikes form for the colors of flower and foliage often clash.

CALYCANTHUS DS Remove some of the oldest wood and thin during April.

CAMELLIA ES A major display plant in the Gulf Region and on the West Coast; some species are tender in the Northeast and need wall protection. *C. japonica* and its many forms are hardy though often flower-bud tender. Dead-heading is desirable on those kinds which do not shed their spent flowers; at the same time trim to shape or restrict growth.

Camellia japonica sports freely and several colors can appear among flowers on one bush. Branches bearing different colored flowers should be traced to their source and

A bottle brush, showing removal of weak growth and of wood that has flowered

Camellias. These should be pruned only to keep the shape

removed. *Camellia sasanqua* and *C. cuspidata* are autumn-flowering species and if pruning is necessary carry this out in April.

Tender species and some of the forms of *C. japonica* may be grown as wall shrubs. Fan train a well-spaced framework and allow side branches to develop just sufficiently to fill the intervening spaces; remove surplus shoots as well as any coming away from the wall.

CAMPSIS D cl These slightly tender climbers need full sun and a south wall. They are strong growers, attaching themselves to supports by climbing roots. Once a well-shaped framework has been trained with the lower part of the wall well-clothed, all side shoots should be cut back in early spring to within two or three buds.

CARPINUS (hornbeam) D T Train to a single leader, feathering until the required length of stem has been produced. Carry out pruning when fully dormant, for if delayed until the sap starts to rise bleeding will follow. Coral spot can be a troublesome disease both on dead and living wood.

CARYOPTERIS D S Unless the wood is thoroughly ripened, die-back is common. In April cut back all young shoots to a framework which is best trained on a short leg.

CASTANEA (chestnut) D T *C. dentata* not recommended in the Eastern states due to sure loss to chestnut blight, but may be grown out of disease range. Other castanea species are not susceptible to the disease. In the garden these are sometimes grown as specimen trees for their deeply furrowed bark is pleasing. Select a central leader and feather until a sufficient length of trunk has been achieved. With age, wood becomes brittle and trees shed large limbs. The spread, therefore, of mature limbs is best reduced by periodically shortening large branches.

CATALPA (Indian bean or cigar tree) D S/T Most often trained as a large shrub with several leaders; when established, keep the center of the bush open. All species form small trees and if desired as such should have a single leader, with side branches reduced and gradually removed. Pruning, when necessary, is carried out in early spring when the old seed pods are removed. When grown for their colored foliage pruning should be moderately hard.

CEANOTHUS D/ES The "lilac" of California, where it is very common. All evergreens are tender elsewhere and the deciduous kinds reasonably hardy.

The evergreen kinds can be, and are often, grown against a wall. Plant from containers and ensure that plants are not root-bound. It is usual to train a parallel framework to cover the wall, ensuring as always that the lower parts are kept clothed. Prune after flowering, cutting only the young growth hard back to the framework. If treated as free-standing shrubs, they are trained to several leaders and trimmed each year, following flowering, back to this framework; winter damage is removed and some thinning may be desirable. Avoid cutting into old wood as this is slow to break.

The deciduous kinds flower on current season's growth which is cut down to ground-level or to a framework in spring.

CEDRUS (cedar) EC Young trees are triangular in outline but with age all develop flat tops. Training of cedars is often neglected as the many badly-shaped trees about the countryside witness. Select and retain a central leader, removing any competition, multiple leaders, or strong growth that develops from low down.

CELASTRUS (bittersweet) DCl These are strong climbers best suited to growing over trees where they can be left to their own devices. If space is restricted, annual thinning is necessary to keep them within bounds; this is best carried out in July when it is easier to recognize dead wood.

CEPHALOTAXUS EC Some kinds tend to sprawl and rather drastic pruning in April may be necessary to correct this.

CERATOSTIGMA ES All species are somewhat tender, but though they may be cut back to ground-level in a cold winter they usually break away freely so long as the

roots are undamaged. Flowering is on current season's growth and all growth surviving the winter is cut back to ground-level in April.

CERCIDIPHYLLUM DS/T In the wild this makes a large tree sometimes with several trunks. Ideally a single leader should be selected, the side shoots being reduced and gradually removed. If a multi-stemmed trunk is required, head the sapling back to 3 ft. at planting and select the strongest three shoots, training each as you would a single leader. More often this is treated as a shrub in gardens and trained to a single leader with all side shoots retained. Some thinning may be desirable and, if space is limited, trimming back of young growth in March.

CERCIS DT It is not easy to train and retain a single leader but this is the best method. Reduce side shoots and gradually remove them. *Cercis* is grown either as a shrub or a tree with little pruning. It is, however, important to train in a satisfactory framework and give a light trimming after flowering to remove the immature seed pods. The production of these can be excessive and if left will reduce vigor and extension growth.

CHAENOMELES (Oriental quince) DS These are spur-bearing shrubs and once regular flowering begins, little pruning is required. Select several leaders and train to a well-balanced framework. An encouragement to help in producing spurs is to cut back all side shoots to three or four buds in the winter months. It is important to keep the center of the bush open and any shoots intruding should be removed.

If grown as wall shrubs to gain some protection for the precocious flowers, they are trained fan-wise. All side shoots are then shortened and after the spur system has formed no further pruning should be required.

CHAMAECYPARIS (false cypress) EC There are many species and a great number of cultivars of varying sizes, shapes and color; no attempt to prune to shape should be made. Many of these cvs produce several leaders, which can easily be overlooked when the tree is young for then they in no way spoil the shape and are usually hidden by foliage. In their early years these are no trouble, but with age the leaders fall away and spoil the outline; unobtrusive wiring is necessary to pull them together. The dwarf and small-growing kinds need no pruning.

CHIMONANTHUS (winter sweet) DS Although fully hardy this shrub does not flower freely unless the wood is properly ripened. For this reason, and to obtain some protection for its flowers during the winter, it is usually grown against a wall. Trained fan-wise, the framework is tied to supports, and all branches coming away from the wall are removed. In July all side branches are cut back to two or three buds of the main framework. In a wet summer any excess growth should be thinned at the end of August to encourage better ripening.

Free-standing shrubs are trained to several leaders and all side shoots are shortened back to two or three buds in July.

CHOISYA (Mexican orange) ES This shrub may be damaged in a colder-than-average winter, so plant in a position protected from cold winds. Dead-head following pruning, trimming to shape at the same time. Does well in California.

CISTUS ES All species are tender to some extent, needing full sun and a well-drained, not too rich soil. Following flowering, remove dead flowers and their stems as well as any winter damage, and trim to shape.

CLADRASTIS DT A large growing tree which should be trained to a single leader and feathered. The wood tends to be brittle and a mature tree can shed limbs, so during training space well the main branches and do not allow undue extension.

CLEMATIS D/ECl If space permits, these climbers can be left to their own devices with a minimum of pruning; most of the species are treated in this way.

They fall more or less into two groups. Those flowering on current season's growth, eg the *jackmanii*, *lanuginosa* and *viticella* groups. These can be cut down to ground-

level in February. To extend the flowering season, some stems can be left unpruned either in their entirety or reduced in length. These shoots should be removed completely in the following year.

The second group flowers on short growth from stems produced in the previous year. Included here are the *patens*, *florida* and *montana* groups. These are pruned after flowering, when shoots which have carried flowers are removed and there is a thinning of excess growth. The *florida* and *patens* groups sometimes produce a late flush of flowers and such shoots are reduced following flowering.

One or two species such as *C. recta* and *C. heracleaefolia* are non-climbers; the former is usually cut to ground-level each February while the second is cut back to a framework.

CLERODENDRUM DS Many species are tender and even the hardiest are frequently cut back in a cold winter though they break away again readily from below ground-level. Cut out winter damage and reduce the shoots in May. Does well in Florida.

CLETHRA D/ES The deciduous species are hardier than the evergreen and have a suckering habit; there should be a thinning out of shoots at ground-level in March. The evergreen group need a favored position to succeed and are usually trained to a single leader but all side shoots are retained.

COLUTEA DS/T If it is to be grown as a tree, train to a single leader and feather. Following the formation of a framework, some thinning may be necessary and trimming of the branches will remove the old seed pods. If space is limited or if they are growing beyond their allotted space they can be cut hard back periodically in winter. When grown as a shrub, train to three leaders. During the winter months cut back hard to a framework and thin out growth from the center of the bush.

CONVOLVULUS ES *C. cneorum* is slightly tender and needs planting in a warm sunny position. Thin out shoots in April and trim to shape

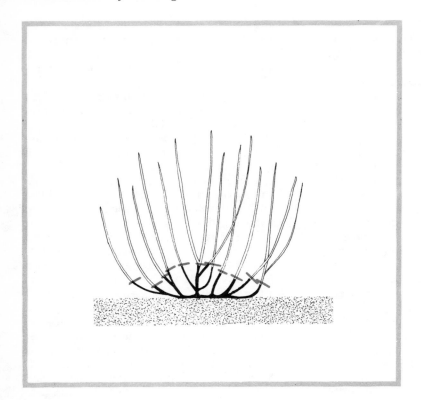

Pruning for bark effect. In this case the pruning is of the type used for those plants whose young growth produces colorful bark in winter. These include several *Cornus* species and several willows *(Salix* species).

CORNUS DS For pruning purposes this genus can be divided into those that sucker and those that develop a single stem. The former tend to make clumps and these should be thinned out during the winter when all shoots which have carried fruit can be removed. A number of these shrubs have attractively colored stems which are cut to ground-level annually in March.

A single leader should be selected for the kinds which become trees; side shoots should be reduced but retained as long as possible.

CORONILLA ES Some species are tender and need protection. Prune in April, trimming back shoots to about half their length.

CORYLOPSIS DS Flowers are produced during the winter on one-year-old wood. No pruning is necessary unless one wishes to restrict growth, in which case prune after flowering.

CORYLUS DS/T A few species are tree-like and these are trained to a central leader and feathered. Suckering along the trunk is common and these should be rubbed off while still soft in May. Mostly the species are shrub-like with a strong tendency to sucker; these are trimmed after flowering to restrict them, and the suckers are also removed. *C. avellana,* the hazel, and *C. maxima,* the filbert or cob, are grown in coppices for their nuts, and *C. avellana* may be cut down to ground-level every few years for brushwood. Both the hazel and cobnut are grown in gardens for their winter catkins; some trimming is needed following flowering. Both have purple-leaved forms which are pruned quite hard after flowering.

COTINUS (smokebush) ES *C. coggygria* and *cotinoides* may still be better known under their classification of *Rhus*. If grown for their smoky flowers there is little pruning except to thin out crowded shoots and to tip shoots in the winter months. When growing the purple-leaved forms of either species for autumn color, hard pruning in the winter months can be practiced.

COTONEASTER E/DS/T   The strongest-growing kinds such as *C. frigida* can be trained to a single leader and feathered so as to form trees. There are one or two pendulous forms such as *C. salicifolia* which can be trained as weeping standards. A single leader is trained up a stake and all side shoots pinched back until there is a clear 6-ft. stem. Sometimes they are high grafted onto a 6-ft. stem. Cut back all side shoots in April and train in a well-spaced framework.

Cotoneasters grown as shrubs only require thinning and restriction of growth; evergreens are pruned in April and the deciduous kinds in winter. The prostrate forms which are used as ground cover benefit from an occasional thinning to let in the light. One or two species, such as *C. horizontalis,* lend themselves to training against an east- or north-facing wall. Form a well-spaced framework, removing any branches which come away from the wall and thinning out the young branches without destroying the grace of the natural habit.

Fireblight is a troublesome disease with this genus.

CRATAEGUS (hawthorns) DS/T Almost all kinds will form small trees if trained to a single leader and feathered; they are, being small in stature, well suited to training as standards. Following training, the only pruning necessary is to remove crossing branches and to carry out thinning during the winter months.

Those to be trained as shrubs can have three leaders. Subsequent pruning consists of keeping the center of the bush open and carrying out judicious thinning in March.

This genus is susceptible to fireblight disease, the symptoms of which are most obvious in June.

CUNNINGHAMIA EC   Train to a single leader, retaining most of the side branches as long as possible. These are produced copiously and some thinning may be desirable. In some forms there is a multiplicity of leaders formed and trying to restrict to one alone is virtually impossible. Such specimens should be trained as shrubs but their centers should be cleared of the mass of dead and weak shoots in April.

CUPRESSOCYPARIS LEYLANDII EC This hybrid is fast growing, well anchored and is much planted in exposed conditions for windbreaks. Plant shrubs from open ground rather than from containers. Select and retain a single leader.

CUPRESSUS (cypress) EC   Most species are tender. Select and retain a single leader, shortening back the side branches on the kinds that spread. In general no trimming is necessary and all side shoots should be retained as long as possible.

CYDONIA (quince) DS   Suckers are freely produced so it is better to train the framework on a short leg. Flowering is on spurs and once established no pruning is necessary, but in the early years side shoots can be shortened back to two or three buds from the framework. Ensure that the center of the bush is kept open.

CYTISUS (broom) DS   Prune after flowering, cutting back to where new shoots are breaking. Avoid cutting into old wood. At the same time cut out crowded shoots and open up the center of the bush.

C. battandieri is so different from other brooms that one may be excused for thinking it a different species. It is slightly tender and often grown against a wall. Either as a wall shrub or free standing, it needs little pruning except for cutting out winter damage in April. Thin and cut out some of the old wood occasionally.

DABOECIA (Irish heath) ES   Shear over the bushes in April, taking off old flower stalks and most of the last year's growth; trim to shape at the same time.

DAPHNE E/DS   In general these shrubs are left unpruned. *D. mezereum* is an exception for if left unpruned it becomes gaunt with long bare stems. Each spring remove those twigs which have carried the flowers. If the prostrate kinds develop long bare stems, these should be pegged down and covered with soil: they will root and, in time, form dense clumps.

DAVIDIA (dove tree) D T Select a single leader and reduce the side shoots, gradually removing them until there is a clear stem of the desired length.

DECAISNEA D S This shrub has a stool-like habit, developing upright shoots which last for several years. When these become gaunt and bare they should be removed by cutting off at ground-level in autumn. Young growth is liable to damage from late frosts and if so affected should be trimmed with a knife.

DEUTZIA D S Pruning follows flowering, when the shoots which have carried flowers are removed. Open up the center of the bush and cut out shoots that are crowded.
   D. scabra is a strong upright grower and has the added attraction of an interesting bark. Leave unpruned, carrying out judicious thinning only.

DIERVILLA D S Following flowering, cut back to where new growth is breaking and thin.

DIOSPYROS D S/T The strong-growing forms are trained to a single leader with side branches shortened but retained as long as possible. The less vigorous kinds can be allowed to remain as shrubs, trained to a single leader or to several. *D. kaki*, the persimmon, is often grown against a wall where the benefit of the extra warmth helps in the ripening of the fruit. Train the main framework as a fan and shorten back the laterals in April.

DIPELTA D S All are strong upright growers which are best left unpruned for their barks provide some interest during the winter. When pruning is necessary, eg in the small garden or when restriction is desirable, do this after flowering, and cut back to where new growth is breaking.

ELAEAGNUS (oleaster) D/E S/T The strongest growers can be trained as small trees by selecting a single leader and feathering. Later pruning is to thin and trim. The less vigorous growers are allowed several leaders and trained as shrubs. Most are grown for their foliage and all benefit from annual pruning. Deciduous kinds should have side shoots cut hard back in March and the centers of the bushes kept open. Evergreens should be pruned in April when they may be thinned and trimmed to shape. As some of the variegated forms have a tendency to revert, any plain green shoots should be removed at their point of origin.

ENKIANTHUS D S Carry out dead-heading, thinning at the same time.

ERICA (heath) E S Only the European species are commonly grown in gardens and one or two of these are tender. Annual pruning is necessary to keep the clumps tidy, compact and floriferous. Using shears, remove old flowers and most of the previous year's growth; the winter and spring flowerers should be clipped after flowering and the summer and autumn flowerers in February. Those with colored foliage can be cut again as the flowers form, for flower and foliage color do not always blend.

ERIOBOTRYA JAPONICA (loquat) D T Widely used around Miami, Florida, as a free-standing plant producing good, edible fruit. The loquat is too large to train against a wall but it is grown as a free-standing small tree for its attractive, large, dark-green leaves. Pruning consists of removing any blackened foliage and thinning in April.

ESCALLONIA E S Hardy in Zone 8. Flowering is on current season's growth and once a framework has been formed, prune hard to within two or three buds of this. In cold districts and for the definitely tender species wall cultivation is necessary. After training a well-spaced fan of branches, cut back all laterals hard in May.

EUCALYPTUS E T Extensively planted in California. Plant small container-grown specimens in an open site but protected from cold winds. A mass of shoots will be produced on the sapling, but eventually one will develop more strongly to become a

Forsythia flowers on wood of the previous season's growth. To ensure an abundance of this type of growth it should be pruned hard immediately after flowering.

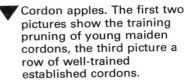

▲Training pruning of young feathered trees. The first picture shows the removal of the lower branches, the second picture the shortening of the laterals to encourage the stem to thicken, and the third picture the removal of a developing double-leader.

▼Cordon apples. The first two pictures show the training pruning of young maiden cordons, the third picture a row of well-trained established cordons.

Salix alba, one of the most spectacular of the willows grown for their winter bark, shown in the first picture. To achieve this, the plant needs to be pruned really hard each spring (second picture).

Removing a double leader. If a double leader is allowed to develop, sooner or later the crotch will collect water, rot and the tree literally split itself down the middle.

Summer pruning a pear tree. This operation is fully described in the text.

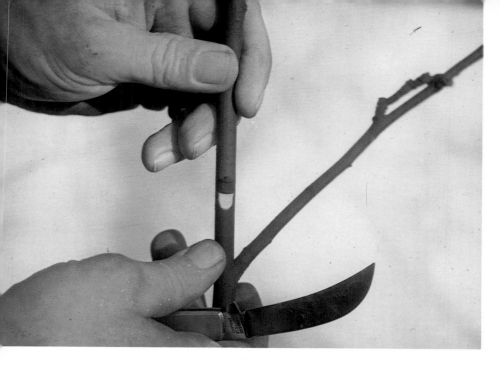

Notching a young apple. The point of this operation is to encourage the branches to grow more horizontally than they would otherwise. It is usually used in training cordons.

Black currant. These can be severely pruned as shown here. When cut to ground level they will produce plenty of young shoots, but will not usually fruit well until the second year after this type of pruning.

A well-kept hedge is a joy in any garden. Modern powered hedge-trimmers now make it relatively effortless to keep a hedge neatly trimmed.

Pruning evergreens. Most evergreens should be pruned in May. Care should be taken not to cut the leaves, as they will brown where cut.

De-horning a pear tree.

leader while the remaining side shoots will die away. Later, branches are shed to leave a clean bole.

Eucalyptus has two stages of growth, juvenile and adult; the shape and color of leaves at each stage may be quite different. Foliage is much in demand by the floral arranger, the juvenile foliage usually being the more popular. Cutting of foliage can take place at any time of the year except when in active growth, but excessive cutting should be avoided during the winter months. When adult shoots are cut the new ones arising will be juvenile and a tree can be kept in this state indefinitely by regular hard pruning in early May.

EUONYMUS D/ES/T A few species will make trees and these are kept to a single leader, the side branches being shortened and gradually removed. The shrubby kinds are allowed several leaders and in general little pruning is necessary except to thin, trim and keep the center of the bush open.

The deciduous kinds are sometimes grown primarily for their autumn color and these can be pruned more severely to encourage strong young growth; this is carried out in March. The best know evergreen is *E. japonicus,* of which there are many variegated forms, some of them very prone to reversion. This species, which is grown mainly for its foliage, is trimmed to shape at the same time as the other evergreens are pruned, in April. This species is very prone to attacks by mildew which can become so bad that normal spraying gives little control. If this happens, severe pruning will remove the unsightly foliage, and the new growth, it is to be hoped, will stay clean.

EUPHORBIA ES While most of this genus is herbaceous, a number are woody. These produce upright, rather succulent stems copiously from a rootstock. After flowering cut out at ground-level all shoots which have flowered and all weak stems. When growth is not strong carry out dead-heading, cutting out completely some of the oldest stems.

EXOCHORDA DS These have a suckering habit and are best trained on a short leg before branching is permitted. Pruning, when necessary, should follow flowering; thin crowded shoots and trim to shape.

FAGUS (beech) DT Often slow-growing in the years following planting, but when once established there is plenty of vigor. Select a central leader, and feather. Weeping varieties are grafted and a leader should be trained up a stake until there is a sufficient length of trunk.

FATSHEDERA LIZEI ES This hybrid has a rather sprawling habit and may be trained up a north or east wall or used as ground cover. Pruning is rarely necessary.

FATSIA ES Remove dead leaves in April and cut out any bare gaunt shoots at ground-level.

FORSYTHIA DS Hard pruning encourages growth at the expense of flowering so annual pruning should be no more than the removal of crowded shoots from the center of the bush and a proportion of the oldest wood. When pruning an old or an extra large shrub, spread the operation over three years; begin by removing the oldest wood and, as new growth is produced, this can be tipped in early summer.

F. suspensa is often grown against a wall where its long pendulous shoots are displayed to better advantage. A well-spaced fan-shaped framework is trained and tied and from this will develop the long weeping branches and stems. These are cut hard back to the framework following flowering. When desired as free-standing shrubs, several are planted together so as to give each other support. After planting, reduce the shoots by half or even more; the following winter cut back to where they begin to curve over. Once a rigid framework has been formed shoots can be allowed to develop freely; subsequent pruning is to remove some or all of the shoots which have flowered.

FOTHERGILLA DS Slow-growing shrubs of bushy habit which need little pruning. Old shoots which become gaunt and untidy should be removed completely following flowering.

✕ *Fatshedera lizei* forms a rather straggly plant unless pruned regularly

Fatsia japonica, showing where pruning cuts should be made to keep the plant bushy

FRAXINUS (ash) DT Train to a single leader and feather. Train in a new leader if the original is lost, remembering that because of opposite buds two will develop where there was one. Weeping forms must have the leader tied to a stake; a clear 12-ft. stem should be produced before a framework is allowed to develop.

FUCHSIA DS Only *F. magellanica* (Zone 5) is hardy enough for cultivation out of doors all the year round and many fuchsias are grown in California. Even those can be cut down in a cold winter but the bushes usually break away freely from ground-level. In May prune back all one-year shoots almost to ground-level or to a framework.

GARRYA (silk-tassel) ES Male and female flowers are produced on different plants and it is the male kind with the long catkins that is grown in gardens. Pruning consists of thinning and trimming to shape in April.

Although hardy if given protection against cold winds, it is frequently planted against a wall where there is some protection for the winter catkins which then grow longer. After training in a well-spaced framework, some trimming should be carried out in April.

GAULTHERIA ES Many species are small growing or prostrate and need almost no pruning. Even the taller kinds require little attention beyond cutting out some of the oldest wood and trimming to shape in April. *G. shallon* is often used as game or ground cover and if it becomes untidy it can be cut hard in April.

GENISTA LS Pruning is generally unnecessary except to dead-head and trim to shape at the same time.

GINKGO BILOBA (maidenhair tree) DC There are many different forms of this tree.

The pruning of fuchsia

It is important to see that pruning is related to the habit of the tree for it is not really possible to change the type of growth. Train to a single leader and feather, taking out strong branches which tend to develop low down on the tree.

HALESIA DT/S Strong growers that will make trees if restricted to a central leader, when feathering will be beneficial. Often trained as large shrubs, when several leaders may be allowed. Annual pruning is minimal and consists of removing crossing branches and keeping the centers of bushes open.

HAMAMELIS (witch hazel) DS Pruning is generally unnecessary. Most kinds offered for sale are grafted, so watch for suckers; as these closely resemble the desired plant remove all shoots coming from below ground-level.

    H. japonica arborea will make a small tree if trained to a single leader; shorten the lower shoots but leave them as long as possible.

HEBE ES A large family tree from New Zealand of varying hardiness, size and form, often as important for foliage as for flower. A number are tender and should be planted at the foot of a wall. Those that flower early in the year, eg *H. hulkeana*, are pruned after flowering when all shoots which have carried flowers are cut out and there is some trimming. Autumn-flowerers are pruned in May when shortening of the shoots is practiced and some thinning.

    The hardy kinds need little attention except a trimming to shape in April.

HEDERA (English ivy) ECl Ivy comes to mind at once when it is a matter of trying to decide on a climber for a wall. It can, however, be invasive and if left unattended can dislodge slates, gutters and down-pipes.

    Ivy has two stages of growth: the juvenile with angular leaves and climbing roots, and the later stage when side branches without roots are produced, leaves become rounder and flowering takes place. It can be slow to start growing up a wall. Train a well-balanced framework, paying attention to clothing, especially at the base of the wall.

Cut well back from windows, doors, pipes, gutters and the roof. When branching starts, these should be cut hard back to the wall in April; it is only the young shoots with roots that stick themselves to the wall and once these die there is no hold. Each year cut out some of the oldest wood so that the ivy cover does not with age become so heavy that it falls away from the wall.

    Controversy has long ranged as to whether ivy growing up a tree is harmful to it. As long as the tree is in good health no damage is done.

HIBISCUS DS Mainly a tropical genus; only *H. syriacus* and *H. rosa-sinensis* are commonly seen in American gardens. This flowers on current season's growth, and once a framework has been trained all young shoots are cut back to within a few buds of it in April. Coral spot can be troublesome, especially when the shrub is not growing well.

HIPPOPHAE (sea buckthorn) DS/T Male and female flowers are borne on separate bushes and so to obtain berries they are often planted in groups with one male to four or five females. Though most often grown as shrubs, they make small trees if trained to a single leader with the lower side shoots reduced. Little pruning is required except to trim and thin during the dormant season.

HOHERIA D/ES Grown in Southern California. All species are tender to some extent and are frequently trained against a wall in all but the warmest districts. Once trained, only removal of winter damage and thinning and trimming in May are required.

HYDRANGEA E/DS/Cl Hydrangeas often take a year or two to settle down before they start to flower regularly. In general they are little pruned except to dead-head and thin out growth in April.

    Climbing hydrangeas attach themselves to their support by means of roots, and as with ivy there are two stages—juvenile growth which clings tight to its support and, where the support has been covered, branching growth with the production of

Ivy, showing where to cut to
keep plants compact

flowers. These flowering shoots are cut back hard in April.

H. macrophylla, the common hydrangea, flowers on one-year wood and pruning consists of the removal of all or part of the shoot which has flowered and the cutting out of weak shoots. In wet seasons a more drastic thinning may be necessary to help ripen the wood. The old flower heads are often of interest throughout the winter and, as in cold districts they give protection to overwintering flowerbuds, pruning can be delayed until April. A few kinds, eg *H. paniculata,* flower on current season's growth and these are cut hard back to a framework or to ground-level during March.

HYPERICUM (St. John's wort) DS A few species are tender. Flowers are produced on current season's growth and in April all shoots are cut to within a few inches of the ground. Larger plants can be produced by thinning and tipping the young growth.

ILEX (holly) D/DS/T Hollies are often slow to establish but having done so, grow very strongly. The strong growers which are to become trees should have a single leader selected but all side shoots retained until they die naturally. Pruning consists of trimming to shape in April. Neglected hollies or those disfigured by leaf miner can be cut back in April or in July. It is preferable to carry out this operation over two or three years rather than all at once.

JASMINUM E/DCl/S Some species are tender and need protection. Both the climbers and free-standing shrubs need little pruning except to remove some of the wood which has flowered. This can be carried out after flowering with most, but for those that flower over a long period pruning should be done in April. *J. nudiflorum* should be pruned after flowering, removing most of the wood that has flowered. This increases flowering and keeps the climber tidier.

JUGLANS (walnut) DT Train to a central leader and feather. Prune when in leaf, since the tree bleeds less then. Young growth is susceptible to damage by late frosts which may necessitate trimming and retraining of a leader.

JUNIPERUS (juniper) EC Some forms make trees and these should be trained to a central leader, with all side shoots retained. The bushes can have several leaders but in April the centers should be cleared of the clutter of shoots, dead and alive. Dwarf and prostrate junipers are not pruned.

KALMIA ES Very little pruning except for dead-heading. When bushes become straggly or there is an excess of old wood, hard pruning can be practiced during April.

KERRIA DS Flowers are produced on the previous year's growth of bright green stems, so attractive in winter. Kerria has a suckering habit, forming large clumps which may need to be restricted. Cut out old canes at ground-level as flowers fade.

KOELREUTERIA DS/T A strong grower trained as a tree by selecting a central leader; the lower branches are retained as long as possible though reduced.

KOLKWITZIA (beauty bush) DS This bush can be left to develop naturally except for the thinning of shoots where crowded. If, however, space is limited, annual pruning can be carried out in June when shoots which have flowered are cut out.

LABURNOCYTISUS DT Flowers should be pink, but on the same tree yellow laburnum flowers and purple broom flowers also appear. At flowering time cut away the shoots bearing yellow flowers for these grow away at the expense of those with pink flowers which will decline unless given this assistance.

LABURNUM (golden chain) DT Most commonly grown as small trees and often trained as standards, for which they are well suited, although a single leader is to be preferred. Strong vertical shoots tend to

appear from low down on the tree and these should be removed as they appear.

Laburnum responds well to spur pruning so that trees can be restricted in size by cutting back side shoots to two or three buds in the winter; they are well suited to pleaching. The trees seed heavily and the immature seed pods should be removed, especially as the seed is poisonous.

LARIX (larch) DC Select a single leader, replacing if damaged by pests or weather, and retain all side branches as long as possible. Prune when fully dormant. Late pruning results in excessive gumming.

LAURUS (bay) ES/T Slightly tender and susceptible to damage from low temperatures or exposure to cold winds. Train to a central leader, retaining all side branches as long as possible. Bays are commonly seen trimmed, an operation which is carried out in April.

LAVANDULA (lavender) ES A few species are tender and need the base of a warm south wall. These are trimmed to shape in May, when winter damage is cut out.

Common lavender is frequently seen in gardens as an untidy sprawling bush, due entirely to lack of pruning. During April, just prior to growth commencing, bushes should be clipped hard, in the course of which old flower spikes are removed and most of the previous year's growth. Neglected bushes need very hard pruning but it is better done in two or three stages and not all at once.

LAVATERA (tree mallow) DS Slightly tender shrubs needing full sun and a rather poor, well drained soil. Trim to shape in April.

LEDUM ES Pruning should be unnecessary except to thin and to remove dead wood. If this becomes excessive it is an indication that all is not well.

LEIOPHYLLUM ES Classed with the heathers which it closely resembles, it is treated in the same way. Trim over with a pair of shears in March.

LEPTOSPERMUM (tea tree) ES Hardy to Zone 9. Pruning is best carried out after flowering, when wood which has flowered is removed together with any winter damage. Some thinning of blind shoots is desirable.

LEUCOTHOE ES Occasionally it may be necessary to remove at ground-level old wood and any unsightly stems in April.

LEYCESTERIA DS *L. formosa* is planted for game cover but is also an attractive addition to a garden for flowers, fruit and stem color. It has a stool-like habit and the old stems are cut out in April. If growth is strong, the entire clump can be cut down to ground-level each fall.

LIBOCEDRUS EC No pruning should be necessary once a single leader has been trained.

LIGUSTRUM (privet) E/DS Privets are best known as hedging plants though specimens are sometimes used in topiary. Grown for foliage, flowers or fruit they can make handsome shrubs or even small trees. Shrubs are left to develop several leaders and established pruning consists of trimming to shape and thinning in March. Strong-growing forms can be trained to a single leader with all side shoots retained but shortened, and eventually removed.

LIPPIA (lemon verbena) DS A tender shrub, usually given wall protection. Even there, it will be cut back in a cold winter. Pruning is carried out in May when the previous year's shoots are shortened almost to a mature framework.

LIQUIDAMBAR (sweet gum) DT Select a strong central leader and feather. Strong branches can occur low down on the tree and these should be removed.

LIRIODENDRON (tulip tree) DT Select a central leader and feather. Remove any strong upright growth which begins from low down on the tree; the bark is easily damaged if blunt tools are used and such wood tends to die back. Training and subsequent pruning is best carried out in July or August.

LONICERA (honeysuckle) D/ES/Cl Shrubby honeysuckles should, after blossoming, be trimmed to shape and the branches which have flowered should be removed. If a feature is to be made of the berries, pruning should be delayed until the winter, or April for evergreens.

It is not necessary to prune climbers every year unless space is restricted. Climbers can be separated into two groups: those flowering on current season's growth are pruned in the winter, when necessary, cutting back hard to a framework; those flowering on one-year-old wood are pruned after flowering when those shoots which have flowered are removed, together with crowded growth.

LUPINUS (lupin) ES Select a site in full sun in a well-drained, not too rich soil. Deadhead and trim to shape annually.

LYCIUM (box thorn) DS All species are slightly tender and liable to damage in a cold winter, so are more commonly grown by the sea. Bushes tend to sprawl, a condition aggravated by too good planting conditions or by planting in shade. Trim drastically to shape in April and thin.

MAGNOLIA E/DS/T Branches tend to be pithy and bark is easily damaged if blunt or badly set tools are used. Pruning is best carried out in July when new growth is complete: dormant wood is slow to heal and die-back following winter pruning is common.

Tree magnolias should be kept to a single leader on which the side shoots are shortened and eventually removed. Young growth is frequently damaged by late frosts and if the leader is destroyed a new one will have to be trained in.

Magnolia grandiflora and many other magnolias are common free-standing trees in the southeastern United States. *M. grandiflora* is often grown in England as a wall shrub although it is really unsuitable in such a position for its large leaves cause undue shading, and with age the trunks become increasingly difficult to keep tied back. Wall-trained *M. grandiflora* does perhaps flower more abundantly than a free-standing tree so if training is undertaken for this reason a well-spaced framework must be provided. This can be fan-shaped or in tiers, ensuring that the base of the wall is kept clothed. Established pruning means removing heads and thinning and cutting away shoots coming from the wall in May.

Bush magnolia need little attention, although dead-heading is desirable for many kinds produce copious quantities of fruit which, if left to develop, reduce vigor. When dead-heading, cut rather than break off the spent flowers for the new growth buds are just behind the flowers. *M. soulangiana* varieties have a tendency to produce masses of young growth along the main stem; this should be rubbed off as it appears.

MAHONIA ES Several of the low-growing kinds can be used for ground cover, which can be kept low and thick if sheared off just above ground-level every three or four years; if not growing strongly remove some of the oldest stems and trim back remaining growth. Other forms need only occasional pruning when the oldest stems are put out at ground-level in April.

MALUS (crab apple) DT Some species are raised from seed and therefore on their own roots, but many species and all cultivars are grafted on to one of the fruit rootstocks which controls the ultimate size of the tree. Most crab apples are trained as standards although they can also be trained to a central leader. Once the framework has formed, there is little pruning required beyond the removal of crossing branches.

MESPILUS (medlar) DT The enjoyment of the fruit of medlar is an acquired taste at present out of favor and this plant is now grown mainly as an ornamental. Once a framework has been formed, either as a standard or with a central leader, all that is necessary is to remove crossing branches.

MORUS (mulberry) DT Select a central leader and reduce all side shoots, gradually removing them. Once a framework has formed, all that is necessary is to remove crossing branches in autumn.

MYRICA E/DS Grown for fragrant foliage and wood, requiring only a trimming to shape in April.

MYRTUS (myrtle) ES All species are tender and need a sheltered garden in one of the milder parts of the country if they are to be grown as completely free-standing shrubs or small trees. Select a central leader and reduce side shoots; retain these as long as possible, removing them if they become crowded. During May, trim to shape and thin out crowded shoots.

In colder areas, myrtle can be grown in the protection of a south wall, either planted close to it and trained against it, in tiers or as a fan, or planted a little way from the wall and allowed to grow free-standing but in its shelter. In May trim to shape and thin out crowded shoots.

NANDINA (heavenly bamboo) ES If old stems become gaunt and leaf size diminishes, they should be cut out at ground-level in April.

NEILLIA DS Shrubs with a stool-like habit. The oldest wood should be removed at ground-level during the winter months and tall stems reduced in height.

NOTHOFAGUS E/DT Hardy on the West Coast as far north as the Seattle area. *N. procera* and *obliqua* are the hardiest species and fast growers, making large trees. Select a central leader and feather; the main branches in the crown should be well spaced.

Most species, being evergreen, are tender and really only suited to the milder parts of the country. Select a central leader but retain all side shoots for as long as possible.

NYSSA DS/T Native to the eastern United States, occurring from Florida to New Hampshire. They will form trees and as such should be trained to a central leader which is feathered. Often grown in gardens as large shrubs when they can be permitted several leaders or again restricted to a single leader but with all side shoots retained. Annual trimming or even judicious removal of branches to restrict growth can be practiced in early spring where space is limited.

OLEA (olive) ES/T Tender and needs a sheltered garden in a mild area to succeed. When free-standing it is usually trained to a single leader; side shoots are shortened and retained as long as possible. Some thinning may be necessary. In less favored gardens it is trained against a wall for protection, either tiered or fanwise. In May cut back shoots coming away from the wall, thin out growth, and trim to shape.

OLEARIA ES/T Occurs on the West Coast. Most species are tender and are often planted as free-standing shrubs at the foot of a wall. Those which flower early in the year are pruned after flowering when old flower shoots are removed and the bush is trimmed to shape. Those flowering late are pruned in May, again old flower stalks are removed and bushes are trimmed to shape.

OSMANTHUS ES/T Most species are tender and need wall protection. *O. delavayi* and *O. heterophyllus* are the hardiest, the former flowering in spring, the latter in late autumn. The early flowerers are trimmed after flowering, the late flowerers in May just before growth begins.

OSMAREA ES × A hardy floriferous shrub that should be trimmed to shape after flowering.

OSMARONIA DS Has a suckering habit and eventually forms large clumps. This shrub, which flowers early in the year, should have the oldest stems, and any weak ones, removed after flowering.

OSTRYA DT Select a central leader and reduce side shoots, gradually removing them. Carry out pruning when tree is fully dormant; delayed pruning results in bleeding.

PACHYSANDRA ES Widely grown for ground cover. Pruning is only necessary if stems become bare and woody or foliage thin. Shear over a few inches above ground-level in April.

PAEONIA (tree peony) DS Most species are herbaceous, only a few having woody stems. Occasionally take out some of the old stems at ground-level if they become gaunt; remove dead flowers and fruiting heads after flowering; if seeds are wanted, delay until these have been shed. Towards the end of a wet summer some thinning of lush growth will aid the ripening of wood.

PALIURUS DS An untidy grower which should be trimmed to shape and thinned out in March. Hardy to Zone 6.

PARROTIA DS A shrub for its early flowers and colorful bark, but particularly for its gorgeous autumn color. A strong-growing shrub with tiered branches which can become tree-like. It can be trained to a central leader with all side shoots retained, or it can be allowed to develop naturally. If a feature is to be made of the trunk, feathering must be practiced until a clear trunk of sufficient length has been obtained. *Parrotia persica* produces masses of branches which should be thinned in winter or following flowering. Cut back to a point where there is another branch.

PARTHENOCISSUS DCl Includes Virginia creeper, Boston ivy, and porcelain vine. All are vigorous climbers which attach themselves to supports by means of tendrils on which there are suckers. Unless given plenty of space (as on an old tree) they can be invasive, shutting out light from windows and dislodging slates, gutters and down-pipes. Where possible an annual reduction of growth is desirable, at the least cutting well back from windows, doors, pipes, gutters and roof. Cut out old wood in winter, remembering that it is only young shoots which are able to attach themselves to supports.

PASSIFLORA (passion flower) D/ECl All species are tender and even *P. caerulea*, the hardiest, can be damaged by winter cold. Train a well-spaced framework to cover a wall, then thin out crowded growth and drastically reduce during May.

PAULOWNIA DT These are fast growing when young, producing rather succulent pithy shoots which are easily damaged by cold, especially when not properly ripened. Flower buds are formed in the autumn and carried through the winter with a high mortality rate, survivors opening in late spring. It is only in the mildest parts of the country that regular flowering can be expected and the tree is usually grown for its foliage.

Select a central leader, retraining if it is damaged by frost, and aim to produce a well-spaced framework for the wood is rather brittle. Young shoots that are well fed grow strongly and produce very large heart-shaped leaves. Each year in April, cut all stems to ground-level and reduce the resulting shoots to three or five. Take care not to damage the roots otherwise these will sucker most profusely.

PERIPLOCA DCl A strong, rather untidy climber that needs trimming to shape in March, with thinning and the removal of weak shoots.

PERNETTYA ES A suckering shrub grown for its attractive show of fruits which remain largely untouched by birds. In good conditions it can become rather invasive and some restriction may be desirable; otherwise occasionally remove some of the oldest wood in April.

PEROVSKIA DS A hardy, summer-flowering member of the mint family. Shoots of this shrub often die back to a rootstock in the winter, and as flowers are on current season's growth, the remaining shoots are cut back to ground-level in March.

PHILADELPHUS (mock orange) DS If there is plenty of space, these shrubs can be grown with the minimum of pruning,

Passion flower, *Passiflora* species. These need to be grown in poor soil in a confined space and pruned moderately if they are to flower well

removing blind shoots from the center of the bush and reducing surplus shoots. When space is limited remove branches that have carried flowers and thin out surplus shoots in July.

PHILLYREA ES Trim to shape and thin out if crowded, in April.

PHLOMIS ES Only some species are woody and most of these are slightly tender, needing full sun and a warm position. Cut out or cut back old flowering stems and thin growth in spring.

PHOTINIA ES A most useful plant in the South and on the East Coast. Somewhat tender elsewhere and often grown on a south wall. Valued more for their young red foliage than for their flowers which are not very interesting. In April all growth is trimmed back to about half of that produced in the previous year.

PHYGELIUS DS The tops are often killed in the winter and, in the manner of herbaceous plants, growth is produced from beneath ground-level. If the tops do survive they should be cut away, for flowering is on current season's growth.

PHYSOCARPUS DS Strong-growing shrubs with a stool-like habit. Cut out the oldest shoots, and any that are thin or weak, during the winter. If grown for foliage cut hard to within a few inches of the ground in March.

PICEA (spruce) EC Select and retain a central leader, keeping all side shoots as long as possible.

PIERIS ES Little pruning is necessary except to dead-head, thin and trim. Young non-flowering growth of *P. forrestii* is a brilliant red which fades green as it ages. A second flush of brilliant growth can be obtained by the (unorthodox) practice of trimming back the shoots when the leaves have turned green.

PINUS (pine) EC Some of the naturally dwarf forms produce several leaders, but in general all species should be kept to a single leader which should be retrained if damaged by weather or insects. Prune when fully dormant to avoid excessive gumming.

PITTOSPORUM ES Most species are tender, *P. tenuifolium* being the hardiest of them. Plant in a protected place out of cold winds. Trim to shape in April, cutting out winter damage and thinning.

PLATANUS (plane) DT Fast-growing trees, commonly used in street planting and there often spoiled by lopping. Given plenty of space, they make graceful trees and with age branches sweep to the ground. Select a central leader and feather, aiming to produce a trunk with a clear stem of 15 ft. with a well-balanced and spaced framework.

PODOCARPUS ES/T The smaller-growing kinds tend to be hardier than the tree forms. The former may be trimmed to shape in April, and the latter, in sheltered gardens, are trained to a single leader.

POLYGONUM DCl *P. aubertii,* the Russian vine, is commonly grown for screening. Its rampant habit makes it ideal for this purpose but unless there is plenty of space its invasive nature can be an embarrassment. Each year, in March, remove shoots that are likely to encroach, drastically reduce and thin out, cutting as near to the ground as possible.

POPULUS (poplar) DT Most species are strong growers when young. Select a central leader and feather. If pruning is necessary, carry out in the fully dormant period or bleeding may result. As canker disease, causing die-back and gumming, is troublesome in some areas all pruning cuts should be sealed. Take care not to damage roots; otherwise suckering occurs.

POTENTILLA DS Untidy growers that tend to collect dead leaves and accumulate a mass of dead or blind twigs. Clear out centers of bushes in March and reduce the previous year's growth by a half.

PRUNUS D/ES/T There are many kinds of

Prunus of differing size, shape and habit, and all of them susceptible to silver leaf disease. Pruning of most species is kept to a minimum after building up a framework. Those which make trees are trained to a central leader and feathered.

Japanese cherries are grafted, sometimes low down but most often onto stems of varying lengths. Heads are often one-sided and by judicious pruning this should be corrected so as to produce a well-spaced and balanced spread.

Ornamental peaches, almonds and their hybrids should have a portion of wood which has flowered removed in April. Sometimes they are fan-trained against a wall; after building up a framework, remove shoots which have flowered. *P. triloba, P. glandulosa,* and their forms are also grown against walls, and following the completion of a well-spaced framework, all side shoots are cut hard back to this after flowering.

Some kinds, eg *P. serrula,* are grown for their barks. Train a central leader and feather so as to expose the trunk as soon as possible. There are a number of weeping forms of cherries of various species and cv groups. These may be low grafted but are most often grafted high. Support the main stem with a stake and ensure that there is sufficient length of trunk to allow the pendant branches to hang gracefully. If the main stem is not long enough to train in a leader, reducing the framework until sufficient length has been gained, then train in a new framework. The evergreen species are most often grown as hedges though they can be grown as specimen plants. Keep to a single leader, retaining side shoots and trim to shape in April.

PSEUDOLARIX DC If conditions suit this conifer it can become a tree and as such is trained to a central leader.

PSEUDOTSUGA (Douglas fir) EC A strong grower of tiered habit which is trained to a single leader, retaining all side shoots as long as possible.

PTEROCARYA DT A strong-growing tree, especially when young. Train to a central leader and feather. Retrain a new leader if

the original is lost: young growth is susceptible to damage from late frosts. Prune when fully dormant for bleeding results if cuts are made once the sap has started to rise.

PUNICA (pomegranate) DS A tender free-standing shrub grown for its attractive flowers in Florida, on the Gulf Coast, and on the West Coast. Train a well-spaced framework and cut back young shoots in May, thinning where crowded.

PYRACANTHA (firethorn) ES Grown against a north or east wall, for which its habit is well suited. During training select several leaders, spacing them wide enough apart to allow side branches to cover their allotted space without overcrowding. The main leaders should be secured in position, for though they keep close to the wall they tend to fall away with age. During April, cut back any shoots coming away from the wall, thin out crowded shoots and trim back. As the leaders become old, select and train in new ones; when these are established the old can be removed.

Pyracanthas are perfectly well suited for growing as free-standing shrubs: three or five leaders should be selected and well spaced. In April open up the center of the bush, thin out crowded shoots and trim to shape.

PYRUS (pear) DT Train to a single leader and feather. No regular pruning is necessary beyond the removal of crossing branches. *P. salicifolia,* and especially its weeping form, needs to have the leader secured to a stake and should be trained to an 8-ft. stem before a framework is allowed to develop.

All species of *Pyrus* are susceptible to fireblight.

QUERCUS (oak) D/ET Transplant when quite small as large specimens are difficult to establish. For deciduous species train to a central leader and feather; the evergreens also are trained to a central leader, the side branches being reduced but retained as long as possible. Ensure that the main limbs are well spaced and give a good shape to the crown. Many evergreens are tender and may suffer damage from cold; some trimming may be necessary in May to remove discolored foliage.

RAPHIOLEPIS ES These are spreading, rather untidy growers which should be thinned and trimmed in April. They are often planted at the base of a wall for some are tender.

RHAMNUS (buck thorn) DS In general these shrubs should be allowed to develop naturally, though a few of the stronger species can be trained to a central leader and feathered. During March thin crowded shoots; forms with fancy leaves can be trimmed back moderately hard.

RHODODENDRON E/DS Azaleas, which form a series among the *Rhododendron* species, are included here. There are very many species and hybrids of varying sizes, shapes, habits, shape of flowers and degrees of hardiness. It is important when transplanting to replant to the same depth as previously. Too deep planting has an adverse effect, causing a sickly appearance and the dying out of parts of the shrub.

Many hybrids and some species are grafted and any suckers which arise from the rootstock should be removed as they appear; if left they grow away at the expense of the plant. Carry out dead-heading annually and at the same time trim back any shoot growing out of alignment. With age, some rhododendrons become too tall, bare at the base, or their shape falls away; these can be cut back really hard after flowering.

Bud blast is a disease which kills the flower buds; remove and burn infected buds.

Pomegranate, *Punica granatum*, showing where the pruning cuts should be made

RHODOTYPOS DS Remove each year, following flowering, the oldest shoots and any that are weak.

RHUS (sumac) DS/T Gardeners are warned that some species can cause a skin rash. People vary in their sensitivity to different species but *R. vernix* and *toxicodendron* are most likely to cause irritation. When pruning any species of *Rhus*, wear thick gloves, cover all bare parts of the body and wear overalls.

Tree forms are kept to a single leader and feathered. Shrubs can be left unpruned, thinning out crowded shoots in March. *R. typhina* and *glabra* and their forms are usually grown mainly for their foliage, either summer or autumn; the amount and size can be increased by pruning in the winter to within a few inches of the ground or to a framework.

RIBES (currants) D/ES A few species are tender. Mostly they flower on one-year-old wood, and after flowering the shoots which have borne flowers are removed. Some form spurs and a framework should be formed on a short leg, and well spaced. During the winter open up the center of the bush and cut back young growth to within two or three buds of the main stems. Evergreen kinds are little pruned except to thin, if required, in April.

ROBINIA DT Most species have thorns and sucker freely if their roots are damaged. The wood of some is brittle and trees may shed large limbs in gales. Train to a single leader and feather, ensuring that the main limbs are well spaced and do not extend unduly. Remove any strong shoots which develop low down on the tree.

ROMNEYA (tree poppy) ES Native to California. Rather succulent, behaving often as an herbaceous plant with growth that dies back to a rootstock in winter. It is usually planted against the side of path because its roots like a cool soil, but has the disconcerting habit of disappearing from the place chosen for it and reappearing elsewhere. In March or April, just prior to the commencement of growth, reduce any surviving shoots and cut out any old ones.

ROSMARINUS (rosemary) ES While reasonably hardy, rosemary may suffer in an extra cold winter, and prostrate forms, if left unsheltered, can be killed or seriously damaged in even averagely cold weather. Bushes can be trimmed to shape in April but it is preferable to wait until after the first flush of flowers is over.

RUBUS (blackberry, raspberry) D/ES A few of the evergreen species are tender and need wall protection. Most species have a stool-like or even suckering habit, but some of the deciduous kinds have canes of only two years' duration.

Brambles with colored stems are cut to ground-level in March, and young growth drastically thinned out in established clumps. Species grown for their flowers or fruit are pruned during the winter. If stems are of two-year duration only, those shoots which have flowered are removed; if stems are longer lived, those which have flowered should be cut back.

RUSCUS (butcher's broom) LS Remove discolored shoots and occasionally some of the old wood in April.

RUTA (rue) ES All species are slightly tender and likely to be damaged in a cold winter. All are short lived and replacements should be kept available for replanting. Common rue *(R. graveolens)* is an untidy grower and needs drastic thinning in May.

SALIX (willow) DS/T Willows vary from tiny shrubs to large trees, all liking a moist soil. Strong-growing kinds are trained to a single leader and feathered; smaller kinds can be similarly treated but with all side shoots retained although reduced. There is a tendency for branches to be damaged or lost in gales so space out the main branches; prevent undue extension and avoid narrow crotches.

Shrubs can be treated as already described or can be allowed several leaders. When willows are grown especially for catkins or foliage, best produced on young wood, cut hard back to within a few inches of the base of the previous year's growth, just before growth commences. When grown for their colored stems, cut to ground-level or to within a few buds of a framework in March. Small growing and prostrate kinds are rarely pruned except to remove dead wood or to thin.

SALVIA E/DS Many salvias are herbaceous but a few are shrubby, and of these the majority are tender. These tender kinds should be planted near the base of a south wall, though even here in a cold winter the tops can be killed—new growth, however, invariably emerges from or below ground-level. For this group, any growth which survives the winter should be cut hard back in spring.

Common sage *(S. officinalis)* is widely grown in the herb garden for culinary use, though colored leaf or flower forms may find their way into the flower garden. There are two groups of common sage: those which flower freely and those which flower not at all or but rarely. With the first, cut out all shoots which have flowered and trim to shape in June. The second are trimmed to shape in April when any flowering stems are also removed.

SAMBUCUS (elder) DS During the dormant season cut out old wood and any weak shoots, open up the center and trim back young shoots. Elders with fancy leaves are cut down to ground-level or hard back to a framework.

SANTOLINA (lavender cotton) ES Fragrant shrub with gray-white leaves grown for its foliage rather than its yellow flowers which, however, have some attraction. Unpruned bushes sprawl untidily and are short lived. After flowering, the old flower stems should be removed and the bushes trimmed back. When growing just for foliage, trimming is carried out in April and most of the previous year's growth is removed; a second trimming is desirable as the flower buds appear.

SARCOCOCCA ES Restrict if clumps become invasive; otherwise just cut out old

gaunt stems, or if clumps become untidy shear back to a few inches of ground-level in April.

SCHIZOPHRAGMA DCl A climber which supports itself by producing roots on its young shoots. Space out these shoots as they begin to grow, pointing them in the desired direction; if they grow wrongly they have to be pulled off the wall and cannot be made to refix themselves. Once the support has been covered, branching occurs and flowering begins. Old flower shoots should be removed in March, being cut back as near as possible to the main framework.

SENECIO ES Many species are tender and need protection of a wall; in May remove winter damage and thin out crowded shoots. Free-standing shrubs are similarly treated in April, when they are trimmed to shape, thinned, and old flower stalks removed.

SEQUOIA SEMPERVIRENS EC These trees need plenty of room and protection from wind, for in exposed conditions they tend to lose their leaders and become stunted. Keep and retain a single leader and all side branches, removing any strong branches which develop low down on the tree.

SEQUOIADENDRON GIGANTEUM (Giant Redwood) EC The world's largest tree should not be planted unless there is plenty of space for development and some protection from wind. Select a central leader and retain all side shoots.

SKIMMIA ES Occasionally remove some of the oldest wood and if necessary trim to shape in April.

SOLANUM ES/D/ECl Only a few species are sufficiently hardy for outdoor cultivation and most of these require wall protection. Some climbers are very vigorous and need drastic annual pruning in May when the previous year's shoots are cut back by half or even more, and all excess shoots are removed entirely.

SOPHORA E/DT/S The stronger kinds will

make trees and should be trained to a central leader and feathered; the weaker kinds, while still trained to a central leader, are allowed to keep all side shoots or at the most these are only trimmed. After initial training there is no more pruning needed.

S. tetraptera is tender in its early years, for which reason it is often planted against a wall for protection. In the early stage young branches often interlace and at this stage no pruning is required, but when strong shoots grow out of the tangle some training is necessary. Once the tree has reached the top of the wall, it will be able to withstand a reasonable amount of cold and can be left to grow naturally.

SORBARIA DS A strong grower with a suckering habit flowering on current season's growth. Prune back in March to within a few buds of well-developed framework.

SORBUS (mountain ash) DS/T The less vigorous kinds are allowed to develop several leaders, and pruning aims at keeping an open center. Most kinds are trained to a single leader which is feathered; the smaller trees can be treated as standards. Once a framework has formed, it may be necessary occasionally to cut out a crossing branch. When trees carry large crops of berries which have escaped depredations by birds, the sheer weight of fruit can pull branches out of shape; pruning to correct this condition may be necessary in March. Most, if not all, species are susceptible to fireblight as well as to honey fungus.

SPARTIUM (Spanish broom) LS Its pithy stems tend to be soft and easily damaged if growing in shade or a rich soil. Trim shoots hard back to a framework in April.

SPIRAEA DS Some species flower on one-year wood, eg *S. × vanhouttei* and *× arguta;* these are cut back to where new growth is developing following flowering. Others such as *S. × bumalda* and *S. japonica* flower on current season's growth and are pruned to within a few inches of ground-level during February.

STACHYURUS DS Occasionally remove some of the old wood, preferably in autumn.

STAPHYLEA DS Generally these have a suckering habit. During the winter remove some of the oldest wood, reducing the remainder and trimming to shape.

STEPHANANDRA DS Grown more for the graceful habit of stems and foliage than for flowers. During March remove some of the oldest stems carefully, trimming and thinning the remainder so as to retain the grace of habit.

STRANVAESIA ES Following training, thin out shoots in April if crowded.

STYRAX DS/T The strongest members should be trained to a single leader with all side shoots retained, but thinned if too crowded. The less vigorous kinds can be treated in the same way, or several leaders can be permitted. Prune in March, cutting out crowded branches and keeping the centers of bushes open. Trimming may be necessary in May if late frost causes damage.

SYMPHORICARPOS DS All species have a suckering habit which can be invasive in a good soil; if so, clumps must be restricted. During March, remove the oldest and weakest shoots, thinning the remainder.

SYRINGA (lilac) DS/T If space is not limited, little pruning is required except for dead-heading and the removal of blind shoots from the center of bushes. In small gardens there should be a reduction of some of the shoots and some trimming following dead-heading.

The stronger kinds will make small trees if trained and kept to a single leader; this needs regular attention because of the forking habit of lilac. Most cultivars of lilac are grafted either on to privet or wild lilac; suckers from the former stock are easy to recognize but those of the latter are not, therefore any shoot which emerges from beneath ground-level should be removed at the point of origin.

TAMARIX DS/T Some flower on one-year-old wood and these should be pruned following flowering, the wood which has flowered being removed and the resulting growths thinned. Others flower in late summer or autumn and these are pruned hard in March, being cut back to a framework; some thinning of resulting growth is desirable. The strongest kinds can be trained into small trees by selecting a central leader and reducing side shoots.

TAXODIUM (bald cypress) D C Select and retain a central leader as long as possible. At maturity the natural habit is to produce a number of upright growths which are allowed to remain.

TAXUS (yew) E C Mostly these are trees but there are shrubby species and many kinds of the common yew *T. baccata*, as well as *T. cuspidata*, are shrub-like. Trees are trained to a central leader with all side branches retained though they can be reduced. Bush forms can be similarly trained or several leaders can be permitted. Some trimming to shape in April of these kinds may be necessary, when the center of the bush should be cleared of clutter.

Irish yews can be trained to a single leader but the resulting tree may be too slender and require staking. Often several leaders are allowed but with age these tend to fall apart and some unobtrusive tying together of main stems is necessary to retain shape.

TEUCRIUM (germander) E S Some species are tender and need protection. All tend to sprawl and are untidy growers. In April cut back to shape and keep within bounds.

THUJA (arborvitae) E C Select and retain a single leader, keeping all side branches; some trimming to shape may be necessary in April. Dwarf or small-growing forms are left unpruned.

THUJOPSIS E C Often rather untidy shrubs with several leaders which need some trimming in April.

THYMUS E S The mat types may need occasional attention to remove dead wood but if this becomes excessive the entire planting should be lifted and renewed. Those forming shrubs, eg the common Thyme *T. vulgaris*, are pruned in April when there is a thinning of shoots and most of the previous year's growth is trimmed back.

TILIA (linden or basswood) D T Strong growers requiring plenty of room. Select a single leader and feather, training a well-spaced and balanced crown. When mature some species produce a rather dense crown and rather more drastic thinning than usual may be required here. Most species tend to produce masses of shoots along the length of their trunks. These should be removed by rubbing off while still soft.

TRACHELOSPERMUM (star jasmine) E Cl Some have twining stems and some have roots that attach themselves to their supports. All produce masses of shoots, which if left become an unmanageable tangle. Drastically thin in May keeping only enough shoots to clothe the wall.

TSUGA (hemlock) E C Select and retain a single leader.

ULEX (gorse) L S Spiny shrub of dense habit which produces a lot of dead wood which if left becomes a fire hazard. Prune after the spring flowering, trimming back growth which has flowered and opening up the center and removing dead wood. Trim after later flushes of flowering to prevent formation of seed.

ULMUS (elm) D T Select a single leader and feather, well spacing out the main limbs. Elms have a disconcerting habit of dropping large limbs without warning, so prevent undue extension of main branches. Dutch elm disease has become widespread in recent years and in spite of claims of resistance all species seem to be susceptible. Dead branches within a crown and premature yellowing are signs of trouble, and if the bark lifted on suspect branches discloses beetle galleries (the disease is spread by elm bark beetle) this confirms the disease. Heavily infected trees must be removed and such an operation is best left to qualified operators. Trees lightly infected will respond to lopping of infected branches if these are immediately removed and burnt. Check remaining branches to ensure that there are no beetle galleries.

VACCINIUM (blueberry) E/DS Occasionally some thinning may be required and trimming to shape. This is best done in early spring.

VIBURNUM D/ES A few species are tender and need wall protection. Some of the winter flowerers also need protection for their flowers. Little pruning is necessary but occasionally some of the oldest wood is removed and it may be desirable to trim to shape following a heavy fruit set. Winter flowerers are pruned in April or May; summer flowerers are cut in February or March, and evergreens are trimmed in April.

VITEX DS/T All species flower late and are slightly tender; they are therefore planted against a wall for protection. Flowering is on current season's growth and in April all shoots are pruned hard back to a framework.

VITIS DCl If growing over a tree, no pruning is required. If on a wall, fence or pergola where space is limited, after training in several rods all side shoots are cut back to one or two buds of these in the winter. Do not delay pruning; otherwise bleeding will occur.

WISTERIA DCl/s A very popular and beautiful shrub that is too often planted where there is insufficient space or where no attention is given to pruning. All species are vigorous and if left to their own devices their long trails can dislodge slates, gutter and down-pipes. Following planting, cut back stems by half, and continue to do this each spring until a well-spaced framework has been trained in. In July all young shoots are cut back to four or five buds, and in March these shoots are reduced to two or three buds. This builds up a spur system and reduces extension growth, so encouraging the greatest number of flowers.

A free-standing shrub can be produced from a wisteria. Train in five leaders, cutting back to 3 ft. in the first winter; the next winter cut the new extension growth back to no more than 3 ft. Some support will be necessary and can be provided by attaching the framework, maypole-fashion, to a central leader. Prune all side shoots, as already described, in July and March.

If trained over a tree no pruning is necessary.

ZELKOVA DS/T Select and retain a central leader as long as possible, reducing side shoots but retaining them as long as possible.

ZENOBIA DS These shrubs have a suckering habit. Occasionally remove some of the oldest wood, tipping shoots in March. Dead-head and at the same time cut back to where new growth is breaking.

THE PRUNING
OF FRUIT TREES
AND BUSHES

8
Apples
and Pears

THE BUILDING OF A FRUIT PRODUCTION UNIT

The principles and practice of pruning are put to the test with tree fruits more than with flowering shrubs or hedges. The latter need to be restrained and shaped but a few ill-considered cuts—or even pruning skipped for a year—will not result in lasting harm. The fruit tree is less amenable to the casual approach. To persuade it to produce regular crops from an early age it must be "built" into a fruit production unit—often of unnatural shape—and every piece of growth must be assessed for its ability to increase fruiting potential.

This begins with the tree in the fruit nursery. These days trees of the major fruits are rarely supplied on their own roots. The nurseryman has a choice of rootstocks which limit the vigor of the variety and encourage it to crop at an early date. Thus an apple variety (the scion) is budded or grafted on to a semi-dwarfing or dwarfing root (the stock) of the same family to produce a tree that remains bush size. The gardener is advised to specify a bush tree when ordering apples or pears. Clearly there is no point in having a tall, vigorous tree that requires a ladder for pruning and picking.

The year after budding or grafting, the scion bud sends up a wand of growth; this first-year tree, or one-year-old graft is sometimes called a maiden. These can be purchased by the gardener who wishes to carry out the critical first phase of training which is to secure the basic framework of branches. Alternatively this is done by the nurseryman, and the gardener buys a two- or three-year-old tree at a correspondingly increased price.

Before detailing the pruning procedure it is important to appreciate why a tree must be carefully "built" from infancy. A good fruit-producing unit is a bush form with branches radiating around the trunk at a roughly equal distance apart. These branches should emerge from the trunk as close to the horizontal as possible—that is, approaching an angle of 90° with the trunk. Throughout its development, light and air must have direct access to all parts of the tree, particularly the center, so that complete pollination and ripening take place. A dense tree or one that is allowed to shoot up in columnar fashion is not efficient in the above respects; narrow-angle branches are more likely to split away under the weight of a heavy crop, and conditions in the dense center favor the development of pests and diseases.

The continuing aim of fruit tree pruning—especially of apples and pears—is to keep the tree balanced in shape, and balanced in the proportions of old and young wood. "Cutting back" is too simple a definition of pruning to apply to tree fruits. Such an arbitrary approach will only serve to delay and reduce the yield of fruit. An unpruned tree, if it is on dwarfing stock, will fruit early in its life and keep bearing. But—and this is why we prune—it will soon become crowded with growths, unhealthy, and bear small (if numerous) fruits irregularly.

So the gardener seeks a compromise by building a tree of manageable shape in the early years, and thereafter by selective pruning maintaining the same proportions while it grows bigger.

An important qualification is that different varieties have different natural growth habits which lend themselves to one form of training and pruning rather than another once the framework is established.

Winter pruning of apples and pears can be tackled after leaf fall and is better done early in the winter than late. Similarly a young tree is best planted and cut back in early winter. Summer pruning, which helps to control vigor and exposes ripening fruit to sunlight, is carried out in late July or early August.

We have seen that a tree may be purchased as a "maiden" or as a two- or three-year-old. The maiden comes as a single wand of growth which must be cut back after planting. A bush tree is the only sensible shape for the modern garden and this means cutting back to leave a stem of about 2 ft. 6 in., using a sharp pocket knife or equally sharp shears. From below this cut in the following spring the growth buds will extend as shoots, the strongest just below the cut, the others in descending order of vigor. The top three shoots are retained as prospective branches of the tree. Ideally these branches should emerge at a wide angle from the stem, but it so happens that the topmost bud always emerges at a narrow angle and grows up almost vertically. However, the next bud down makes a better angle, so a way has been devised of rejecting the unsuitable top bud. Before the buds break a small piece of wood is nicked out just below the top bud, so diverting most of the sap energy to buds below. The following winter the stub above the new top shoot is cleanly cut away. If any of the three top buds is close to its neighbor it is best cut out and another lower one allowed to grow.

We have reached the stage at which three shoots—framework branches—have been secured, either in the nursery before purchase or by the gardener. In the winter following their extension each of the three is cut back by about two-thirds. If possible choose a point above an outward-facing bud and always cut at a slight slope away from the bud.

From below this cut at least two shoots can be expected to extend from each parent branch. So the following winter there are six or more branches (six is a good number), which this time are cut back by half their length. One more year's development gives an "adult" tree with an optimum of twelve branches spaced evenly all round, with none growing into the center.

THE AIM OF SUBSEQUENT PRUNING

After this, hard pruning ceases and attention is directed towards keeping a balance between old and young wood. It is important to recognize by looking at the winter buds whether they will make growth shoots or flowers and fruit. Growth buds are slim and pressed tightly to the stem, while fruit buds are fatter and stand more away from the stem.

Look at a branch in winter that has been growing (and been pruned) for three years. The top section will be bearing mainly growth buds, the middle section mainly fruit buds, and the oldest section will have groups of fruit buds called spurs. With the renewed pruning method to be described shortly, this type of branch is kept for several years until replaced by a younger cropping unit. As well as vigorous and potentially useful laterals from the main branches, short and weak growths will also appear. Invariably these should be pruned hard back—by at least two-thirds—for they have no future as replacement branches. It is a safe rule of thumb to prune weak growth hard and strong growth lightly once the tree framework has been formed. Any attempt to control vigorous growth by hard pruning will be met by an even more vigorous response by the tree. On the other hand there is a chance that stronger growth will result from the hard cutting back of a weak shoot.

A sequence showing the pruning of a mature apple tree. The operation is fully described in the text

The following section deals specifically with apple tree pruning. Just as a number of trained tree shapes have become accepted as distinct forms (bush, dwarf pyramid, cordon etc), so a number of pruning methods have been developed to deal with certain training systems or with certain varieties. Essentially these can be narrowed down to two: established spur pruning and renewal pruning. The latter is the more natural approach with a bush tree. However, variety has an influence on choice, and some varieties have growth that lends itself to spur pruning. At the other extreme there are other varieties, which tend to bear fruit towards the tips of branches. Clearly all laterals should not be cut hard back to form spurs, and even renewal pruning entails shortening most shoots. Both methods would reduce the crop to a greater or lesser extent. Thus with these tip-bearers and other very vigorous varieties it is best to restrict pruning to the removal of dead, competing and inward pointing wood each winter.

RENEWAL PRUNING OF APPLE TREES

Renewal pruning suits most bush apple trees. While some varieties lend themselves to a spur pruning system, they can also be successfully pruned by the renewal method. In its simplest form the method involves the winter pruning of some new growth and shoots that have carried fruit. Leading lateral branches are left unpruned in order to develop fruit buds along their length. When they are brought down near the ground by the weight of fruit it is time to replace them. For this purpose a sub-lateral, upward growing and suitably positioned, has been kept lightly pruned. The old branch is cut cleanly away at its junction with the replacement leader.

Shoots are not pruned until after they have borne fruit, but once this has occurred (on two-year-old wood) the shoot is ready to be renewed. This is done by cutting it back to within two buds of the main branch. Renewal of fruiting wood is the aim of the system. Young shoots arising directly (that is, not associated with wood that has borne fruit) are nearly all left unpruned in order to make fruiting wood the following year. But a minority are cut hard back to two buds. Temper this cutting back according to tree vigor. If the tree is vigorous leave a number of these shoots unpruned each year. Hard pruning of nearly all new shoots is the rule on weaker growing trees.

This staggering of shoot pruning helps to overcome the tendency known as biennial bearing—heavy crop one year, none the next.

ESTABLISHED SPUR PRUNING

In contrast to the renewal method, fruit-bearing wood is left to develop a fruiting spur system with established spur pruning, instead of being replaced after fruiting. Each new shoot is cut back according to its vigor: to four or five buds if vigorous, to one or two if weak.

In future years growth shoots from this spur are treated similarly, with the result that a group of spurs consisting almost entirely of fruit buds is built up. Clearly some shoots must be treated differently, and the leading shoots on branches are only lightly pruned by the removal of the top inch or two. And a minority of shoots of medium vigor are not spurred back until they have fruited (which will happen earlier than on spurred shoots).

Vary the number of spurred and unpruned shoots according to tree vigor, spurring weak growth and sparing the strongest. Spur systems get crowded after a few years and themselves need pruning. Thin out up to half of the clusters to allow space for fruit development and light for ripening.

SUMMER PRUNING

Summer pruning is carried out about a month before a variety is picked—say from mid-July to late August—and at such time there should be little if any regrowth from the cut shoots. Its result is to expose fruit and wood to the beneficial effect of light and air; it can reduce pest or disease incidence and will give a check to vigor. Weakly growing trees should not be summer pruned. So shorten new shoots to 3 in. wherever this will expose ripening fruit.

REJUVENATING AN OLD TREE

Old apple and pear trees are often found in a neglected state, and fit at first sight only for grubbing out. However, with remedial pruning over a period of years such trees can be given a new lease on life. Neglect and abuse may have resulted in one of two ways. Where no pruning has taken place for years the tree will be over-grown with worn-out fruiting spur systems. The other possibility is that the tree has been hacked instead of pruned so that it is a mass of congested shoots and quite fruitless.

In the first case, a procedure known as dehorning is adopted. This is drastic pruning and involves cutting out one or two branches each year as close to the crotch of the tree as need be. Initially remove branches that crowd the center, and later thin out the periphery if necessary. Aim to reduce overall height by cutting to a point where a lower branch can take over. Cut cleanly at these junctions (for a detailed account of tree surgery see page 135). If there are not many branches to be removed but spur clusters are crowded on old wood, thin out these clusters by half over a period of some four winters.

A tree that has been hacked to resemble a pollarded willow again needs whole branches cut out before shoot thinning is tackled on the remainder. Encourage a new framework of well-placed branches by selecting some of the best-placed shoots to be new leaders and tipping them. Leave enough of the others as laterals which will make fruit buds if left unpruned. Cut out at their base surplus "water-shoots" from old wood.

PEARS

Fruit spurs form more easily and abundantly on pears than on apples, so that they are well suited to be trained in shapes, such as cordon or espalier, and pruned by the established spur system (described on page 88). Dwarf trees can also be formed without any trouble, along the lines described for apples. With pears it is generally easier to achieve the ideal goblet shape with an open center.

To form a low-growing dwarf from a one-year-grafted tree, allow three well-spaced shoots to develop after cutting back, then double the number by pruning each to two buds. Treat further growth on established spur principles already described.

Summer pruning is of more benefit to pears than apples, and is most important on trees trained to special shapes. The method is to reduce weaker side shoots to four leaves and stronger ones to six leaves in late July. This is followed up by winter spur pruning back to two buds. As with apples, a minority of shoots

Summer pruning of a cordon apple. This is an essential part of the routine shaping of cordon trees

can be left unpruned for a year to ensure a succession of fruit buds.

Leaders need to be cut back by a third in winter (with most apple varieties they are just tipped). Thick spur clusters soon develop on pears and need to be thinned progressively.

SPECIAL TREE SHAPES

Dwarf pyramid

By definition these trees are dwarf and pyramidal in shape. Dwarfness comes from the rootstock. In contrast to an open-centered bush tree, the central leader must be retained to serve as the spinal column of the pyramid. If a one-year grafted plant is planted and then cut back in the normal way, the top buds must be stimulated into strong growth. The top one will be vigorous enough, but the next three or four can be encouraged by nicking out a small piece of bark above each one.

In the early winter of the following year these shoots are pruned back by half, cutting to a bud on the underside so that the shoots tend to grow out at a wide angle. Continue to winter prune the central leader so that it maintains vigorous vertical growth and keep the extension growth of the other main branches in proportion so that the shape continues to resemble a Christmas tree. As the leaders extend, tiers of side shoots will develop. Once the lowest side shoots have borne fruit all side shoots are summer pruned and spurred back in winter as described earlier for apples and pears. A pattern develops of tiers of laterals with sublaterals.

Once the central leader has reached the maximum height desired, the relatively hard winter pruning of leaders ceases.

Cordon

As with other restricted tree forms, trees to be grown as cordons should be on a dwarfing rootstock and of an amenable variety. The various cordon shapes and espalier trees require a supporting framework of posts and wire, which is best set up before the row is planted. Wires can also be fixed directly to a garden wall. There is little point in choosing a space-saving tree form unless several are planted, and this makes economical use of the posts and wire. These must be stout and durable, and wooden posts —even the best looking—will need replacing one day. Angle-iron or old piping is probably best and needs to be sunk deeply or buried in concrete. Concrete posts will also serve, though they tend to be bulky. Use strong wire and intermediate supports every 3 ft. or so. Wires at 2, 3, 4 and 5 ft. from the ground provide a good supporting system.

Best known of the variations on the cordon theme is the oblique cordon, and this is considered the best for the average garden. More space is required by the single U-cordon, which itself can be compounded into a double U-cordon.

The oblique cordon begins life as a single stem and remains thus throughout its cropping life. To form such a cordon of your own, start with a one-year grafted tree and plant it close to the wire at an angle of 45° to the ground. Allow 3 ft. between each tree and plant so that the graft union (visible as a swelling just above the soil mark on the stem) faces the ground. This is done because the base of the tree will be under pressure and the union might split if facing upwards. With each cordon a bamboo cane is required, tied to the wire at a 45° angle, to which the one-year grafted tree is secured with soft string.

The leading growth is allowed to extend each year, and cane and cordon are lowered by about 5° when the top wire is reached. This procedure reduces vigor and leads to plentiful fruit-bud formation. Summer pruning is the main treatment for a cordon. It begins the summer after planting when shoots are shortened back to four or five leaves in late July/early August. In winter they are spurred back further. Thus spur systems develop in the lowest part of the stem and extend upwards each year. By the time most of the cordon is clothed with fruit spurs it is time to practice spur thinning on the oldest.

As always, use discretion in pruning according to tree vigor, cutting back thin weak shoots harder than average and very strong ones less hard. This is a simple and rewarding way to grow apples or pears in a small garden.

To make a single U-cordon, the one-year grafted tree is cut back to about 1 ft. and two resulting shoots are allowed to extend in opposite directions, then tied to stakes on a wire 1 ft. above ground. After about 6 in. of growth has been tied to the stakes the shoots are turned upwards and tied to upright stakes. In winter they are pruned by about one-third. In successive winters they are just tipped, while all side shoots are summer and winter pruned to make spurs. Skill is exercised in keeping both arms of the U at the same height, and there is twice the work in the double U-cordon.

During the next growing season, two more suitably placed opposite shoots on the vertical leader are chosen as the second tier of the espalier, and other shoots in the same region are pinched hard back while young. In this and future years all side shoots from the tiered branches are summer pruned according to vigor, and spurred back in winter.

The formation of each tier follows the same pattern as the first: namely, supporting the opposing shoots first at 45° then lowering them to the horizontal while keeping a balance for vigor.

Single oblique cordons — in this case of "Cox's Orange Pippin," a plant not well known in the United States — showing the short spurs, now in flower, on which the fruit will be produced

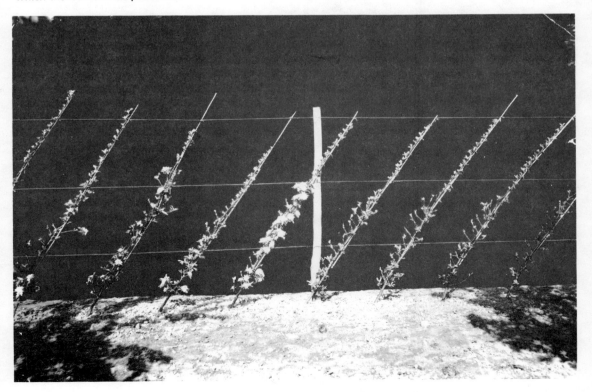

Two fine fruiting cordon apples, showing the very
heavy crops that can be obtained when apples are
grown this way

Espalier

This horizontally spreading shape requires
around 15 ft. of wall or post-and-wire space
per tree. The system is built up in tiers, tapering to the top. A one-year grafted tree is cut
back to about 18 in., to a bud above a pair
lying opposite each other. The terminal bud
and the two below are allowed to grow, the
terminal being tied to a vertical stake on the
wire-supporting framework, the two opposite
shoots to stakes at an angle of about 45° from
the leader in order not to weaken them by
making them horizontal at once. They are lowered to the bottom wire at the end of the first
growing season, but if one is weaker it is only
partially lowered. The vertical leader is winter
pruned back to about 2 ft.

A sequence showing the use of canes in the training of a woody plant which is required to grow flat against a wall. The operation is described in detail in the text

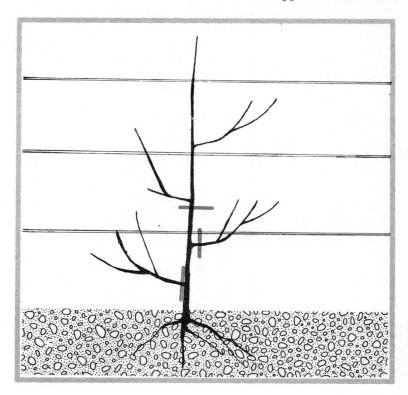

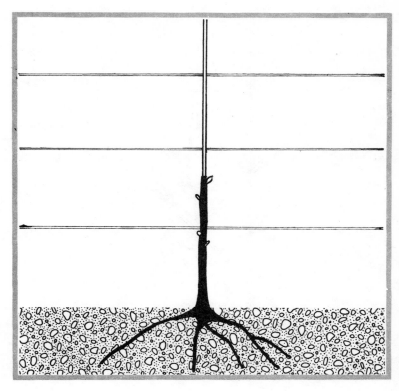

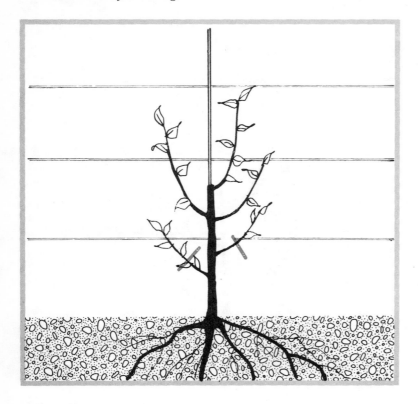

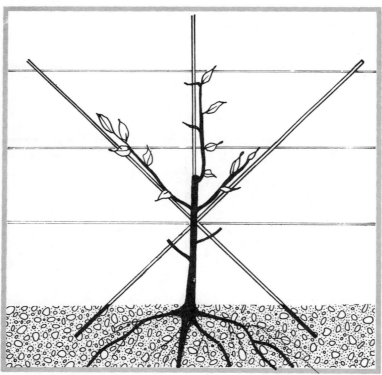

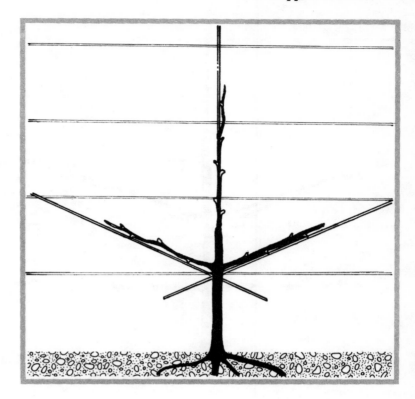

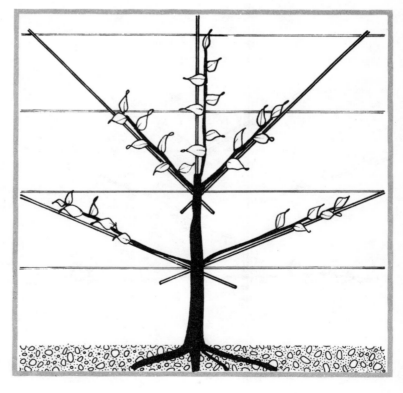

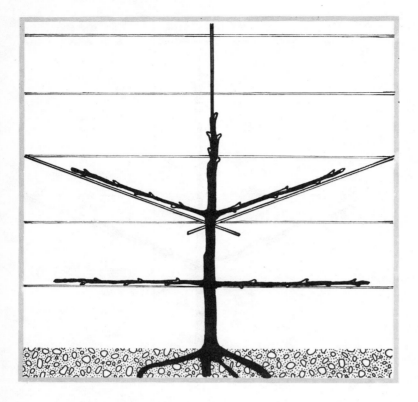

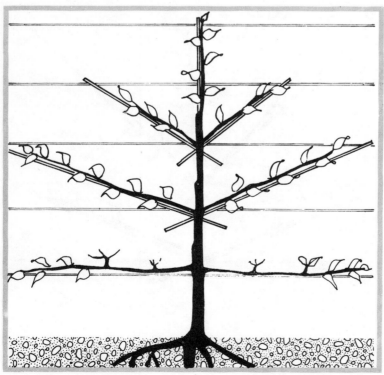

9
Plums
and Cherries

PRUNING RISKS FOR PLUMS

Plum pruning is not without risk—to the tree. The spores of silver leaf fungus disease may gain entry through pruning cuts, and this disease is capable of killing a tree. As the name implies, leaves on affected branches take on a silvery appearance by comparison with healthy leaves.

Suspect the disease if you see much dead wood in a plum tree. If towards the end of the year small bracket fungi are produced on the dead wood it is almost certain that silver leaf is the cause. For confirmation, cut into suspected wood and look for a dark ring staining the wood; this is a sure sign that the fungus is present.

First action with an established plum or gage tree in the garden is to cut all dead branches back to healthy wood, preferably by mid-July, certainly before the end of August. If they prove to be silver leaf infected, cut back until no stain can be seen in the wood. Then paint the cut surfaces with a pruning compound, and burn the prunings immediately.

Because of the risk of introducing this disease, all bush, half-standard or standard plum trees should be pruned as little as possible. What pruning is necessary should be carried out in June or July when the cuts heal rapidly and silver leaf infection is least likely. All that is required is to remove crossing branches that may rub together and a few others that may be crowding the center of the tree. Some varieties have a pendulous habit and the tips of a few branches may have to be cut back. Plums fruit on wood produced in the previous year and on spurs on older branches. If pruning in June or July means the removal of branches bearing unripe plums, the operation can be delayed until immediately after picking.

Plums are particularly prone to branch splitting, especially if the crop is heavy, and it is wise to have some props handy to support laden branches in a good year. However, if the worst happens, remove the broken branch at once and cover all damaged surfaces with wound paint.

ESTABLISHMENT OF A BUSH PLUM

In the average garden a bush plum, with 2–3 ft. of trunk before the branches begin, is the best shape. Half-standards, with a 4-ft. trunk, are useful for the more spreading varieties. Plums are not suitable for growing in restricted forms such as cordon or espalier.

Nurserymen will supply one-year-old trees (maidens) or older trees on which a framework of branches has already been formed. If a two- to three-year-old tree is purchased, no pruning will be required until the spring a year after planting. To produce a bush tree from a maiden, the stem must be cut back to just above a bud, about 9 in. above the desired position of the lowest branch. This is done after planting, in the spring and before bud burst. Small shoots low on the stem can be left, as they help to build up the tree until a number of strong branches have been formed. In July shorten them back to four or five leaves, and after two to three years remove them completely.

Pruning in the second year involves the selection of the main branches. A number of strong shoots should have formed near the head of the tree, and about four of similar strength and evenly spaced round the stem are selected. These young branches ideally should make an angle as near as possible to 90° with the main stem. Such branches will be able to support a heavy weight of fruit, while those emerging at a narrow angle will be weak and prone to split. The chosen wide-angled branches are cut back in spring to a bud about halfway along their length while the remainder which form narrow angles and are badly placed are removed entirely.

In the third year, leaders (strong-growing branches) are cut back by half the growth they made in the previous year, and crossing and crowded shoots are removed. In subsequent years pruning is carried out in June or July and only involves the removal of dead, broken, crossing and crowded shoots as already mentioned.

FAN TRAINING FOR PLUMS AND GAGES

A possible training shape for plums and gages where a large area of wall is available is a fan. Early training is similar to that for peaches, and is dealt with in that section (page 100). But once the framework has been built up and wall space filled, plums are treated differently because they fruit on both old and new wood. All pruning is carried out in the growing season and starts with rubbing out shoots that grow directly towards or away from the wall. Strong-growing upright shoots should be removed when young. Extension growths that are needed to fill a gap or replace an old branch are best taken from the lower side of the older branches and tied horizontally. This reduces their vigor.

Other shoots that are not wanted as leaders should be cut or pinched back in July to five leaves from their base, and are further shortened to a stub a few inches long as soon as the fruit has been picked. At the same time dead wood is removed, while naturally short spurs can be left unpruned.

Plums are naturally vigorous and if fan-trained trees grow strongly without cropping, then root pruning will be necessary. This work is carried out in the autumn and involves digging a semi-circular trench round the tree about 30–36 in. from the wall. Make the trench just over a spade's width and about 18 in. deep. Remove all strong roots that cross the trench, chopping through them with the spade at each side of the trench. When the work is finished the soil is replaced and trodden down in layers a few inches deep at a time. During digging take care not to sever fine feeding roots. If a free-standing plum tree is to be root pruned to check excessive vigor, tackle half the root area one winter, the other half-circle the following year.

BULLACES AND DAMSONS

Bullaces, small wild plums ripening in autumn, and damsons, close relatives which ripen from mid-September onwards, are treated in exactly the same way as plums grown in the open. A good framework of branches is built up in the first few years, and in subsequent years dead and less fruitful old branches are removed, together with any shoots that are crowding the center of the tree.

Both bullaces and damsons live to a great age (fifty years is not unusual) and a neglected old tree can be rejuvenated by cutting most of the main branches back to near the trunk so that new shoots are produced that can be built into a new framework of branches. Always leave at least one large branch to act as a "sap drawer." Spread the work over two years, dealing with half the tree at a time. Spring, just before the buds burst, is a good time to carry out this work, but use a sharp knife to trim ragged cut surfaces, then immediately cover with pruning wound paint.

CHERRIES

There are two distinct types of cherry: the sweet or dessert kind, and the sour cherry. With neither of them is winter pruning carried out owing to the risk of silver leaf infection.

Sweet cherries

These are not suitable for the smaller garden because no dwarfing rootstock is available and consequently they grow into large trees. Picking what fruit has been left by the birds is difficult from a tall tree, and to ensure cross pollination two different varieties have to be planted. A fan-trained tree is the only feasible shape, and this requires sufficient wall space for two trees spaced 18–24 ft. apart. Even so, root pruning may be necessary in order to check vigor. However, birds can be kept from the fruit by draping netting over the tree.

The tree is built up in the same way as the peach (see page 100). Sweet cherries are pruned as little as possible once the framework is formed. Cut side shoots (laterals) back to five or six leaves in July, then shorten these again to three or four leaves in September. Rub out shoots that appear on the wall side of the branches as soon as possible, while they are small. Branch tips (leaders) are not pruned until they reach the top of the wall when they are bent over and tied down for a year. This will

weaken them and encourage new shoots to
break so that the following September the
leaders can be cut back to replacement laterals.
Also in September dead wood is removed and
strong vertical shoots cut out, or tied down
horizontally (which will weaken them) if they
are needed to fill a gap.

Acid cherries

Acid cherries are not as vigorous as the sweet
kinds and bush or fan trees can be planted in
the garden about 15 ft. apart. They are more or
less self-fertile and a single tree will set a good
crop. The framework of bush trees is built up
in the same way as for plums. Acid cherries
fruit mainly on wood produced in the previous
year, so once the framework of the tree has
been formed subsequent pruning is aimed at
encouraging this wood.

These cherries will make fresh growth from
dormant buds in old wood, so each year a few
branches are cut back to two-year-old wood in
the case of young trees (about four or five years
old), and to three- and four-year-old wood in
the case of older trees. This is best done in
April after buds have burst. Diseased and dead
wood is also removed, as well as inward and
crossing branches to keep the head thinned out.
Once again, paint large cuts with pruning
wound dressing to prevent silver leaf infection.

Fan-shaped trees are built up in the same
way as for peaches (page 100), except that only
3–4 in. is left between the side shoots. Once the
tree is established a few of the older branches
are cut back each year to encourage a supply
of young shoots which are tied in 3–4 in. apart
in winter. Otherwise pruning treatment is the
same as for peaches.

Sour cherries can be fan-trained
against a wall to give a heavy
crop in a confined space

10 Peaches

Peaches flower early and the blossom is frequently killed by frost, with consequent loss of fruit. To obtain some protection they are often grown trained in a fan-shape against a south- or west-facing wall. However, in a relatively frost-free situation free-standing trees can be grown with fair prospect of fruit.

A peach needs to be trained fairly flat against a wall to obtain maximum ripening of both wood and fruit

FREE-STANDING BUSHES

Training a free-standing bush is easy enough. When a one-year-old tree (a maiden) is planted, it is cut back in the following May to a suitable side shoot (lateral) 18–24 in. from the ground. Side shoots lower down the stem are removed entirely. In the following year there will be further side shoots which will compose the framework of branches. Cut these back by about one-third to an outward-facing bud. Shoots growing into the center of the tree are removed and dead tips are cut back to a live bud.

The aim is to have branches arranged as evenly as possible in a spiral round the main stem. In subsequent years what pruning is necessary is carried out in May. It is only necessary to tip-prune any shoots that have died back and to remove branches that are crossing others or crowding the center of the tree. When old branches get pulled down to the ground by weight of fruit they are cut back in May to a strong-growing vertical lateral.

FAN-TRAINED TREES

Trees are planted 9 in. away from a wall and the branches are tied to horizontal wires spaced about 6 in. apart so that they radiate like the spokes of a wheel. After planting in February a maiden tree is cut back to 24 in. from the ground. As soon as shoots start to extend, one is left at the top plus a pair 8–9 in. above the ground and close together but on opposite sides of the stem. The other buds are rubbed out with the thumb. The two lower shoots are encouraged to grow along bamboo stakes fixed to the wires and radiating out from the stem at an angle of 45°.

When the shoots are about 18 in. long the main stem above them is carefully cut out. If one shoot tends to grow more strongly than the other it must be brought down to a more horizontal position, which will restrain it.

In the second winter the two shoots are tied down to an even more horizontal position and cut back to about 18 in. In the second summer a shoot at the end of each branch is allowed to grow along a stake to continue the growth of the main branch. Two shoots on the upper side of each branch are also allowed to grow, plus one on the lower side of each branch, and these are also tied to stakes fixed to the wires. All other buds are rubbed out as soon as they can be handled.

In the third winter each new shoot is cut back by about one-third to a growth bud, on the upper side of the shoot if possible. Growth buds can be recognized because they are slender, while fruit buds are fat. If in doubt always cut to a triple bud cluster as these invariably consist of two fruit buds and one growth bud.

If there is space for a large tree, the treatment carried out in the second summer can be repeated once more, but otherwise steps are taken to secure a crop. To this end, third-summer treatment involves allowing the bud at the end of each of the eight branches to grow on, tying them to stakes or directly to the wires. Rub out shoots that grow directly towards or away from the wall. Shoots from the remaining buds on both sides of the branch are kept where they can be spaced about 6 in. apart, and excess buds are rubbed out.

Once the shoots have grown to about 18 in. the tips are pinched out. They are tied to the wires so they are spaced 4–6 in. apart. These shoots should bear fruit the following year.

Fourth and subsequent summers require the removal of superfluous shoots, the pinching back of shoot tips and the tying-in of new shoots that will bear fruit in the following year. To obtain replacements for fruiting shoots, one shoot from a wood bud at the base is allowed to grow. Two shoots can be taken if there is a space to be filled. If the wall space is filled pinch new growths back to four leaves after six or seven have been formed.

Shoots close by a developing fruit are

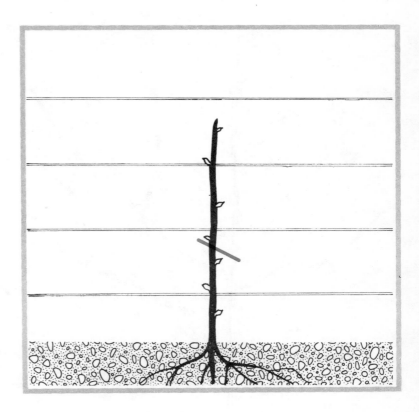

Stages in the shaping of a fan-trained shrub or tree. The sequence shows the same plant in the April of its 1st, 2nd, 3rd, and 4th years

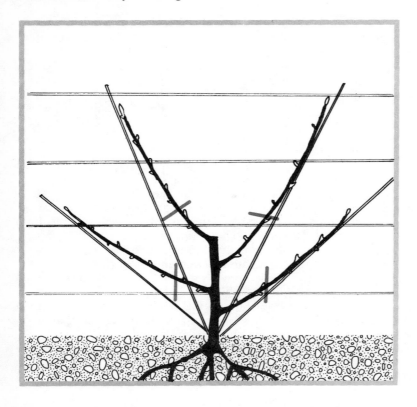

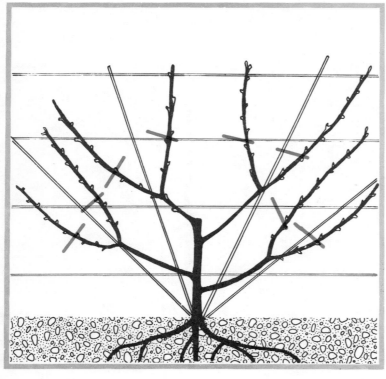

pinched back to two leaves. After the fruit has been gathered, fruit-bearing wood is cut off close to its replacement, which is then tied to the wires. Dead or diseased wood is removed at the same time.

NECTARINES

A nectarine is a peach without the soft fuzz on the skin, and is pruned in exactly the same way. Being more tender than peaches, nectarines are not usually successful as outdoor bush trees.

APRICOTS

This fruit likes a warm climate and flowers even earlier than the peach so that frosts often kill the blossom outdoors. For this reason apricots are generally grown in a fan-shape against

a warm wall and covered with a few layers of fine mesh netting when frost threatens. It is even worth erecting a polyethylene screen round the tree when flowering starts. Hand pollination with a paint brush then becomes necessary. This is a good idea in any case with apricots, which are self-fertile.

Pruning follows the same pattern as for peaches, but as flowers are produced on spurs on older wood as well as on the previous season's shoots, spurs are encouraged by pinching back laterals when they are about 3 in. long.

On rich soils apricots are prone to produce excessively long shoots but few fruits. If this happens, vigor can be checked by lifting and replanting the tree if it is small enough, or by root pruning as described on page 135 if it is large.

11
Grapes

It is easy to regard grapes as an exotic crop for the greenhouse, and to some extent this is true if large dessert berries are desired. But in many parts of the country, a good crop can be obtained outdoors. If the right varieties are chosen these are usually excellent for eating and for wine-making.

VINES UNDER GLASS

The easiest method is to train vines as single cordons, that is with a permanent single stem called a rod, from which side shoots grow each year and bear the bunches of grapes. As the best grapes grow on a current year's shoot, arising from the stub of one pruned the previous year, the pruning method has this end in view.

Young vines are usually planted just outside the greenhouse or conservatory and the main stem taken through a gap in the wall into the house. This is done to provide better conditions for the roots. If it is more convenient, the vine can be planted in the greenhouse but more watering will be required.

A supporting system of horizontal wires is necessary. They must be 9 in. apart and at least 9 in. below the glass to avoid leaf scorching. The vine is planted in winter and cut hard

back. The following season the strongest young shoot is allowed to grow up towards the apex of the house and the others are rubbed out. This leader will produce laterals (side shoots) and these are pinched out at the tip when 18–24 in. long. Sub-laterals (side shoots from the laterals) are pinched when they have produced one leaf. It is important to space the laterals carefully so they are about 18 in. apart on alternate sides of the main stem. Badly placed or additional laterals must be removed while they are young enough to be rubbed out.

The vine will be ready for its first annual pruning when the leaves change color in autumn, just before they fall. Although the rod may have reached the top of the greenhouse in the first year, it should be cut back to a bud where the shoot is well ripened. Cut back the laterals on the rod to one or two buds in order to build up a spur system. The following year one other shoot is allowed to continue extension growth until the roof area has been filled. Laterals are selected on alternate sides every 18 in. and stopped as before. Once this main shoot has grown to its maximum extent it is treated as a lateral.

Returning to the laterals that were cut back

to spurs the previous autumn, these will produce new shoots in spring which, when 1–2 in. long, are reduced to two per spur by rubbing the rest out. If the lowest spurs are slow to produce new growths, spray the rod with warm water on sunny days, untie it from its supports and arch it down close to the ground until growth can be seen.

As they grow, tie the selected laterals to the framework of wires. Flower trusses will soon start to form on them, and further growth is then pinched out at two to four leaves beyond the truss. Sub-laterals are stopped at one leaf. It is usually necessary to reduce the number of bunches so that remaining grapes will swell to a good size. Some can be removed when the flowers are seen to have set, the remainder when the grapes have started to swell. As a guide, work to the formula of one bunch to 9 in. of rod. So that each bunch is not overcrowded, cut out some of the berries with a fine-pointed pair of scissors. The remainder will be larger as a result. Of course, grapes for wine-making need not be thinned as much as those for the table.

The final job in the year's program is to cut the laterals back to about two buds in autumn, leaving only short spurs along the main rod.

VINES OUTDOORS

A south- or south-west-facing wall is an ideal place to grow a vine. A suitable shape is a fan tied to horizontal wires with two or three main rods carrying laterals. Training is the same as for vines under glass, except that initially two or three main shoots are allowed to grow. As before, a spur system is built up with laterals cut back close to the main rods in autumn.

The training method about to be described is suited to vines grown in rows—that is, without the support and protection of a wall—but the method can be adapted to wall training.

Vines supported in rows by wires can give good crops, and if glass or polyethylene screens can be used to help ripening in late summer. The vines are planted 4 ft. apart in a row running north–south or on a south-facing slope. Two wires are stretched along the row at 12 in. and 24 in. above the ground. Plants are set out during winter and cut hard back to encour-

age strong growths in summer. Three strong growths are enough and they will probably have to be cut back again in the second winter until the plant is well established and growing strongly. In the third winter two of the three shoots are bent down and trained along the lower wire. They are pruned back to between five and seven buds. The third shoot is cut back to three buds to produce three strong shoots for the following year.

The two shoots that have been spread out in opposite directions on the bottom wire and tied down will produce laterals from each bud. These will grow up to the top wire, to which they are tied. When the bunches of blossoms are opening (about June) the fruiting laterals are stopped a few inches above the top wire by going down the row with shears.

If berry size is important, the bunches can be thinned when the grapes are swelling, leaving the best bunch on each lateral. Trimming with shears may be needed at intervals during the season to keep growth in check, and unwanted growths along the main stem and laterals should be rubbed out while small. The three replacement shoots are allowed to grow without stopping.

Glass or plastic panels along each side of the row in late summer will help ripening, but leave the top open for growth to come up and be trimmed back at intervals.

Pruning takes place once again after leaf fall when the two fruiting arms are united from the lower wire and cut away close to the main stem, while two of the replacement canes are tied down in opposite directions to the lower wire and shortened as described above. Again, the third shoot is cut back to three buds for three new replacement shoots.

Vines can also be grown under large barn cloches, and pruning is largely the same except that only two new shoots are required each year. One wire only is needed, 9 in. above the ground. One shoot is shortened to eight buds and tied to the wire, while the other is cut back to two buds. These two buds will produce the replacement shoots. Cloches are put over the row in summer. Grapes are produced on the laterals that grow from the shoots tied to the wire. Stop these laterals at two leaves beyond the bunches.

12 Currants and Berries

BLACKCURRANT

Blackcurrant is an easy-to-grow and valuable bush fruit: valuable because it is one of the richest sources of vitamin C, while ease of culture extends to pruning. It also extends to propagating so that there is no excuse for keeping old and unfruitful bushes in the garden. Ten years is a good life for a blackcurrant bush, by which time it is likely to be much weakened by "reversion" virus and the microscopic mite that helps to spread the trouble. Mites hatch within blackcurrant buds which appear abnormally big, giving rise to the condition called "big bud." The tissues in the bud are attacked by the mites and emerge distorted and unable to bear a decent crop of berries.

Control of big-bud mite by routine spraying also limits the spread of the virus, but pruning plays a significant part in the health of the blackcurrant by removal of quite substantial amounts of the oldest wood each year, thus disposing of pest colonies.

Growth buds and roots are produced prolifically by this fruit, and it is the gardener's job to promote those buds best placed to rejuvenate the bush. It follows that basal growth gives maximum renewal, and roots that develop on basal suckers are beneficial. Avoid at all costs the formation of a leg or stem on blackcurrant bushes. Foundations for a good shape are laid when the young bush is first planted by cutting the existing shoots back to 1 in. above the soil. Buds will break below these cuts and send up a cluster of shoots. In the autumn of the same year cut back half these young shoots, each close to soil-level.

Those remaining will bear fruit the following summer. They will also give rise to side shoots destined to fruit the year after, along with the regrowth from the cut-back shoots. In autumn again it is time to prune out a proportion of the shoots that have carried fruit. A reliable rule of thumb is to remove—by cutting out close to the soil—a quarter of the *old* wood each year.

It is tempting to make pruning cuts just above vigorous young growths that arise about halfway up the older wood. But if many cuts are made at this height the bush soon becomes tall, spindly and weakened as the supply of vigorous basal shoots on their own roots dwindles. So be firm and cut low: there will be ample renewal each year to replace the missing top growth. As well as old wood removal, encourage further suckering by cutting hard back about a quarter of the new basal growths each autumn. Pruning to this pattern will give the ideal balance of older and younger shoots.

It is possible to prune the blackcurrant while it is still in leaf without apparent detriment. Commercial growers commonly cut out the fruit-bearing shoots at picking time and take them away for stripping. This serves as pruning also, but such a ruthless approach is not recommended to gardeners.

Suckering and rooting near the soil surface is the aim, and is encouraged by laying mulches of straw, peat or rotted compost over the root area in early summer to keep the soil cool and moist. By the same token it is unwise to cultivate around the bushes and risk severing roots. Just remove weeds by hand if possible or hoe very superficially.

RED AND WHITE CURRANTS

Red and white currants are rarely seen in shops, which is good enough reason to grow them. Unlike the blackcurrant they are grown on a single stem or leg, and in this respect resemble the gooseberry, which also has similar pruning requirements. When cuttings of these currants are rooted, the buds on the bottom 6 in. of stem are rubbed or cut away to leave a clean leg. This will have been carried out on bushes purchased by the gardener. It is sufficient to keep four well-spaced shoots initially at the top of the stem, and to cut these back to three buds in the first winter. The following year a framework of about eight branches will be established.

Unlike the blackcurrant, which fruits only on wood made the previous year, the red and white currants keep making fruit buds on the old wood year after year, so that old wood cannot be cut away without sacrificing a substantial amount of potential fruit. Suckers can arise from ground-level but are best torn away at the point of emergence in order to maintain a vase-shaped bush.

Many side shoots are made and these currant bushes will rapidly become a forest of growths unless pruned in summer as well as winter. This is done in late June, shortening side shoots to within 3–4 in. of the main branches.

Winter pruning consists of cutting the side shoots back further, to two buds or half an inch. This is also the time to reduce the new growth at the top of the main branches. For the first couple of years reduce the new extension growth by a half, but as the bush matures be progressively more severe in limiting its height increase.

Birds like to eat unprotected buds on these currant bushes in winter, as well as sampling the fruit in summer, so it is wise to grow them within a bird-proof fruit cage.

To summarize the pruning process: preserve a clean stem or leg; establish a vase-shaped structure of about eight main branches; shorten back all side shoots in summer and again in winter, and tip-prune leaders in winter. Allow for the occasional replacement of an original branch by a suitably placed younger one.

Red and white currants can be trained as cordon bushes to economize on space in the garden. Wires strained between posts are the

A sequence showing the pruning of a gooseberry bush. Regular, routine pruning leads to larger fruits and heavier crops. It also helps to control some pests and diseases

ideal support. Set the bushes 1 ft. apart sloping at an angle of 45° and tied to a bamboo cane which is itself attached to the wires. Allow only one branch to grow as the leader, which should be tip-pruned back by one-third of its annual extension growth each winter. Prune all side shoots to 4 in. in summer, then cut back to half an inch in the winter. Fruit will form in a column on these spurs. Cordon currants are less attractive to birds because they do not provide a good footing.

GOOSEBERRY

Gloves are essential when tackling gooseberries with shears, and are also advisable at picking time. Garden bushes are grown on a clean stem or leg and, as with red currants, a semi-permanent framework of branches is established. However, the gooseberry fruits on both one- and two-year-old wood, so that removal of a proportion of old wood each year will not jeopardize fruiting.

If the bush is pruned on a replacement system rather like the blackcurrant, it is likely to fruit heavily, but these fruits will tend to be small and most suitable for bottling. If, on the other hand, a spur-pruning system is adopted, such as was described for the red currant, there may be fewer fruits but they will be large and of dessert quality.

So, if size of berry is not important, winter-prune the bush by cutting out at a low level the older central wood in order to open up the bush and make picking easier. New growth on the chosen leading branches should be cut back by a half. Pruning for quality involves summer pruning of all side shoots to 4–5 in., followed in winter by "spurring back" to 2 in. From then on, regrowth from these spurs is cut hard back to base. Limit the number of leader branches to a maximum of eight, and in winter cut back the annual extension growth by about half. Gooseberry varieties that have a dropping habit should be leader-pruned to counteract this tendency. Always make the cuts on the leaders to an inward and upward pointing bud. As with red currants, birds will go for the buds in winter and it is best to keep gooseberries in a fruit cage.

The great advantage of cordon training for the gooseberry (apart from being space-saving) is that picking is made so much easier. Training and pruning follows the pattern already presented for red and white currants. It makes

good sense to grow both types of fruit on the same framework.

Note: In the United States there are restrictions on growing currants and gooseberries where white pine is prevalent. It would be advisable to consult your state agricultural college about restrictions in your area before planting.

RASPBERRY

Autumn is the best time to plant new raspberry canes. Once planted they are pruned back to 1 ft. from the ground, cutting just above a bud. The following year these canes will be developing their root systems and sending up new canes. It is these that bear the first crop of berries the following summer.

It is best to provide raspberries from the outset with supporting wires stretched between posts. The first flush of new canes the summer after planting should not be pruned, although weak ones are best removed. The original canes are cut out at ground-level that autumn.

Regular pruning and thinning out begin in the second summer. More new canes than are required are produced along the row, and weak ones should be cut out or hoed away when they can be distinguished. Make a point of removing those furthest from the parent canes in order to keep the row narrow and easily supported. As a rule of thumb, keep six at the most from the group that has sprung from the parent root.

Treatment of canes that have carried fruit is simplicity itself. Cut them all out at ground-level soon after picking, and burn them as a precaution against spread of disease. Then, having selected and retained the best of the new canes, these are tied securely but not tightly to the wires. A continuous looping run of soft string is a good way to secure them.

February is the time to tip-prune the new canes, removing the top 3 in. This is done partly to remove damaged tips and partly to stimulate fruiting shoots below.

With the autumn-fruiting variety September fruit is borne on the current season's growth and new canes must be cut down to about 4 in. above ground in February–March.

LOGANBERRY

A loganberry is generally trained in a fan-shape against a wall, fence or post-and-wire framework. After autumn planting existing cane is cut back to 9 in. above ground. Two or more new growths should arise at ground-level the following year. These are spaced and tied to horizontal wires with soft string. The following year these canes will bear fruit. The main pruning operation consists of their complete removal after picking.

The loganberry grows vigorously and a disciplined approach to training is required to prevent its becoming unkempt. By the time the first fruit-bearing canes are cut away there will be a flush of new growths. The weakest can be removed at once and a maximum of eight strong ones tied down fan-wise on either side. Secure them so that the center of the fan is left open to receive the following season's new growths. These in their turn will be lowered to re-form the fan when the older ones are cut out. This effectively separates old and young canes each year, and also ensures that the young growths are "above" the old ones and so are less liable to be infected by any disease spored on the older parts.

In March the tips of the canes which wave above the top wire (5–6 ft. high) are cut off. Growths that sprout an inconvenient distance from the parent root should be cut away at an early stage. These and blackberries are thorny subjects and gloves need to be worn during training and pruning operations. If planting for the first time take advantage of the thornless varieties of both fruit that are available and which are much easier to manage.

BLACKBERRY

The pruning and training approach described for the loganberry can be applied to the blackberry—though this fruit is even more precocious in its annual growth and needs a firm hand to keep it within bounds. It bears fruit on the same wood for several years but it is best to cut out growths after they have fruited.

In the second year lead the fruiting canes up and along the higher wire of the supporting framework, while the new growths are grouped together and tied in at the bottom. In their turn a selection of these will be trained upwards when the older ones are removed at the base after fruiting.

OTHER HYBRID BERRIES

Certain hybrid berry fruits are offered by nurserymen, most of which are akin to the loganberry or blackberry, while other have currant *Ribes* in their parentage. Generally they are less hardy and less vigorous than their cousins. They may indeed be damaged by hard frost. Examples are the boysenberry and youngberry. The wineberry is attractive in growth but has fruits of poor eating quality. Maintain a balance of fruiting and replacement growth in all cases.

Early stages in the training of a blackberry cordon. Note the way the canes are tied securely to the wires, and that the wires are kept taught

Currants are most easily controlled
when grown as cordons. Not only do
they seem to fruit better due to the
benefit of the extra light that reaches
them, but it also makes picking the
fruit easier

Pruning a blackberry. This cordon-
trained plant has been cut hard back
to its framework canes in late
autumn. Fruit will be borne on young
growths emerging from these canes in
the spring

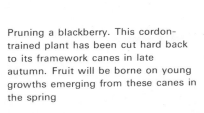

HEDGES, GREENHOUSE PLANTS, AND THE CARE OF OLD TREES

13
Hedges

While the pruning of shrubs and fruit trees is a matter of choice—they will continue to "perform" if left alone—it is a necessity with hedges, which must be tailored to shape. The term "pruning" is not often used by the gardener when he clips or trims the hedge, but that is what he is doing. The cuts are aimed at restricting or redirecting growth, and that is **what** pruning is all about.

A hedge is a barrier, or at least a demarcation. However low or slim, tall or spreading, its function is to separate one area from another, and to do it as harmoniously as possible. When kept under control a hedge is pleasing to the eye because it is a unity, the individual plants lost in a network of growth. Left untended, the unity that makes it a hedge is lost, and it resembles more a row of unkempt trees or shrubs too closely planted.

The degree of growth varies greatly, however. More often than not a formal feature is desired which is regularly trimmed into a neat oblong shape, an elongated pyramid or a loaf of bread outline. A well-managed hedge of this type is evenly textured from ground to top. The opposite is not uncommon—a bare base, a matted middle and a sparse, spindly top. The informal hedge, as the name implies, can be

Three examples of the training of hedges into formal shapes: loaf shaped (this page), elongated pyramids (opposite page, top), neat oblong (opposite page, bottom)

114

An informal hedge of mixed shrubs. Such hedges need only occasional pruning to remove all the spindly growths

Viburnum tinus, showing the best shape to which to prune it for hedging purposes

treated with a laxer discipline. It is enough that growth should be fairly even. Flowering shrubs are chosen, and are permitted to extend their flowering shoots naturally.

A well-maintained hedge costs less than a fence or wall in the long run. It filters wind, so avoiding the dangerous turbulence caused by solid barriers, and the effort of training is amply rewarded by the natural beauty.

Choice of hedging material is extensive, yet the majority of gardens still display only the well-know kinds. We do appear to live in a world subdivided by privet and berberis (barberry). In fact the choice is wide enough to give great variety in height, leaf color and texture, flower and berry. There are a large number of suitable evergreens.

The approach to pruning is governed by the nature of the hedge. With small-leafed plants (which are chosen for formal hedges), overall trimming with shears or powered trimmer is the rule. When treated informally, however, pruning is more selective. With large-leafed subjects, such as laurel or rhododendron, prune with hand shears. The effect of large leaves

severed by hedge shears is unsightly and such treatment causes the leaf edges to discolor. There may be times when drastic measures are necessary in order to thin out and revive a hedge. At such times, when old wood must be severed, a narrow-bladed saw is the best tool.

A basic rule relating to hedge shape is this: prune so that the bottom is wider than the top. This allows the whole surface area to get an equal share of light. All parts then grow evenly and the base does not become bare.

Many gardeners willing to use fertilizer and manure on other plants neglect to feed hedges. This is a serious oversight for a hedge must occupy the same ground for many years and the mass of roots below the closely set plants make heavy demands on the food reserves of the soil. Only a well-nurtured hedge will respond properly to pruning, so dress the root area every two or three years with balanced organic or inorganic feeds applied in the spring. To reduce the risk of pests and diseases be sure to clear away debris below the hedge each spring.

Begin pruning as soon as a newly planted hedge is established and making growth. To get

Hedge shears. The most important thing about hedge shears is that they should be kept really sharp. The design is rather less important

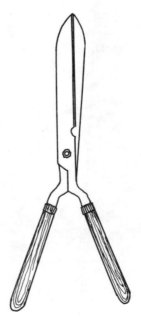

The blades of shears should be laid flat against a hedge when it is being trimmed

The training of a topiary tree. Any clippings should be removed from beneath the tree and replaced with a top dressing of manure or compost

The shaping of a young hedge. The aim is to make the hedge narrower at the top than at the bottom. If the sides of the hedge are vertical the shoots at the base will not receive sufficient light to make enough dense growth

the desired well-clothed base, clip off at least half the length of the new shoots three or four times each year until the young hedge is evenly dense. After this it will need attention once, twice or perhaps three times a year. It is the ubiquitous privet that demands the most trims. If privet and thorn are to look their best, three trims are generally needed, starting in June with follow-ups at six-week intervals. The relatively slow-growing yew and lonicera need several light trims if they are to keep a close finish.

August is the month to give the single annual clip that is enough for a great number of hedging plants—beech among them. The table which follows (pages 122–3) summarizes the best available hedging subjects, and the pruning treatment for each is given in the following section (page 128–9).

Tools for hedge trimming must be in good condition. Shears that are blunt or out of alignment will tear growth and give an unsatisfactory finish—to say nothing of leaving the gar-

dener tired and frustrated from unrewarding effort. Likewise see that pruning shears cut evenly and without effort. Both can be professionally sharpened during the winter. A power-driven trimmer must be maintained as befits any electrical appliance, and great care taken in its use, especially if it is cable-trailing rather than battery powered.

Cutting a hedge straight by eye is not easy. A good aid is a tight line stretched between posts of equal height to indicate the topmost level of cut. On relatively short lengths, two canes alone pushed into the ground to equal height will suffice. A hedge tapering to a narrow top is the easiest shape to trim, as well as being best for growth. Always hold shears and power trimmer flat against the surface: never poke the tip into the hedge. Be sure to cut back long shoots that "fill a gap." Being cut they will branch and fill the gap better. Always shake the hedge to dislodge clippings, and clear them from the base.

Powered hedge trimmers: though frowned upon by many people as not very good for hedges this is in fact a fallacy, and if you have large areas of hedges to keep trimmed these powered tools are probably the most efficient way of doing it

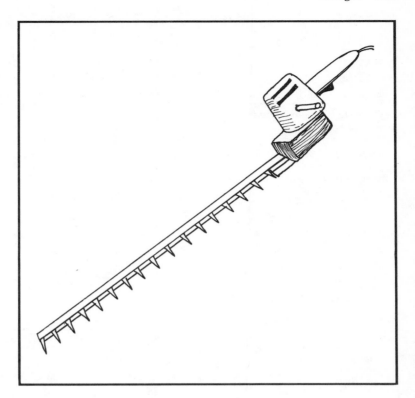

Stretching a line in order to obtain a straight, level line across the top of a hedge

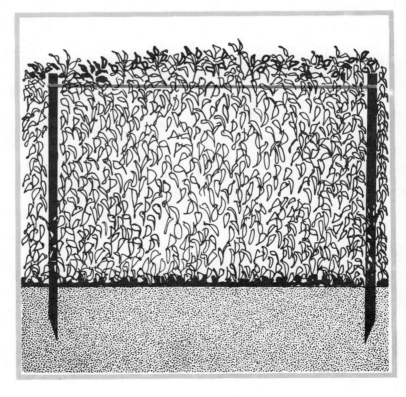

Hedges and how they perform

NAME	LOW OR HIGH	FORMAL OR INFORMAL	EVERGREEN OR NOT	FLOWERS AND/OR FRUIT
Beech (Fagus)	H	F	semi E	—
Barberry (Berberis) darwinii	H	I	E	FF
x stenophylla	H	I	E	FF
thunbergii atropurpurea	H	I	NE	—
thunbergii 'Atropurpurea Nana'	L	F	NE	—
thunbergii erecta	L	F	NE	—
verruculosa	L	I	E	FF
Box (Buxus) edging	L	F	E	—
Handsworth	H	F	E	—
Chamaecyparis lawsoniana (forms 'Allumii' and 'Fletcheri' have bluish-grey foliage)	H	F	E	—
Cotoneaster lacteus	H	I	E	FF
simonsii	H	I	semi E	FF
X **Cupressocyparis** leylandii	H	F	E	—
Cupressus macrocarpa	H	F	E	—
Escallonia	**H**	**F**	**semi E**	**Fl**
Euonymus japonicus (good variegated forms; attractive fruit on some)	H	F	E	—
Hebe or Veronica	L	I	E	Fl
Holly (Ilex)	H	F	E	Fr
Hornbeam (Carpinus)	H	F	semi E	—
Laurel, Portugal	H	F	E	FF
Laurustinus (Viburnum tinus)	H	F	E	—
Lavender (Lavandula)	L	F	E	Fl
Lilac (Syringa)	H	I	NE	Fl
Lonicera nitida	L	F	E	—
Myrobalan plum (Prunus cerasifera)	H	I	NE	Fl
Olearia haastii	L	I	E	Fl
Osmarea 'Burkwoodii'	H	I	E	Fl
Pittosporum tenuifolium	H	I	E	—
Potentilla "Farreri'	L	I	NE	Fl
Privet (Ligustrum) (golden form also)	H	F	semi E	—
Prunus 'Cistena' Crimson	L	F	NE	Fl
Dwarf Prunus cerasifera 'Nigra'	H	I	NE	Fl
Blaze Prunus cerasifera 'Pissardii'	H	I	NE	Fl
Pyracantha rogersiana	H	I	E	FF
Quickthorn Crataegus	H	F/I	NE	FF

Rhodendron	H	I	E	Fl
Rose, HT and Floribunda vars, esp Queen Elizabeth	H	I	NE	Fl
Rose species	H	I	NE	Fl
Rosemary (Rosemarinus)	L	F	NE	Fl
Santolina chamaecyparissus	L	F	NE	Fl
Sea Buckthorn (Hippophae)	H	I	NE	FF
Snowberry (Symphoricarpos)	H	I	NE	FF
Lilac (Syringa)	H	I	NE	Fl
Thuja plicata	H	F	E	—
Yew (Taxus)	L/H	F	E	Fr

Low	under 4 ft. naturally		NE	not evergreen; leaf loss in winter
F	formal (naturally regular or easily pruned to that shape)		semi E	retains a proportion of foliage in fresh or dead state
I	informal (looser habit, usually flowering)		FF	flowering and fruiting
E	evergreen (but may apply to silver or other colored foliage)		Fl	flowers attractive
			Fr	fruit attractive

Yew is a classic hedging plant, and is ideal for formal shapes. Care should be taken that the trimmings are not left where livestock can reach them since they are poisonous

Hippophae rhamnoides, the sea buckthorn is sometimes grown as a hedge and is stunning in fruit. Both males and females must be planted to obtain fruit

A rosemary hedge showing the more rounded shape to which it is best adapted when grown as a hedge

A lavender hedge. Although often grown rather in the manner of box edging, lavender is really best trained in a low mound when grown as a hedge

A badly trained hedge. Typical of what happens when the sides of the hedge are vertical. The hedge is bare at the base, matted in the middle and very spindly at the top

Euonymus japonicus will not stand rigid pruning and would be best used as a semi-formal hedge

Hebe makes a useful low growing, but rather informal hedge

Berberis darwinii is one of the
best barberries for hedging
purposes. It is covered in
attractive golden yellow flowers
in spring and bears an
enormous crop of fruits in
autumn

A lonicera hedge showing the
best shape for pruning such a hedge

How and when to prune hedges

Beech	trim to keep dense and regular in late summer or winter; brown leaves stay on through winter
Berberis darwinii	lightly after flowering in spring; flowers form berries later
Berberis x stenophylla	lightly after flowering in spring; flowers form berries later
Berberis thunbergii atropurpurea	lightly to restore shape in winter (after autumn foliage effect)
Berberis thunbergii 'Atropurpurea Nana'	does not exceed 2 ft.; trim in winter to maintain formal shape
Berberis thunbergii erecta	lightly in winter; makes a narrow hedge
Berberis verruculosa	lightly to restore shape after flowering in spring; flowers form berries later
Box	lightly as required in spring and summer
Chamaecyparis lawsoniana and forms	leave leading central shoot uncut until desired height is reached; use shears to limit spread in late summer
Cotoneaster lacteus	lightly to restore shape in summer, with regard to winter berry effect
Cotoneaster simonsii	trim this semi-evergreen lightly to shape in winter after berry and leaf effects have been enjoyed
Cupressocyparis leylandii	leave leading central shoot uncut until desired height is reached; use shears to limit spread in late summer; this is a fast growing conifer
Cupressus macrocarpa	as above
Escallonia	lightly in spring, and again after flowering in summer to encourage more flowers; except near the sea, frost may cut back this shrub
Euonymus japonicus	use shears to avoid unsightly cut leaves; lightly to maintain shape in spring
Hebe or Veronica	trim to shape in spring; can be cut back hard if getting leggy
Holly	lightly to restore shape in late summer, with regard for winter berries; cut back regularly when young to keep bushy at base
Hornbeam	as for beech above
Laurel	use shears to avoid unsightly cut leaves; cut to maintain shape and density in spring
Laurustinus	lightly in summer with shears
Lavender	lightly in spring, and cut off dead heads after flowering
Lilac	as little as possible with shears after flowering
Lonicera	frequently when young to achieve basal thickness; when mature, in spring and summer as required to maintain shape
Myrobalan plum	frequently when young to achieve basal thickness; when mature trim twice in summer
Olearia	lightly after flowering in summer
Osmarea	lightly after flowering in summer
Pittosporum	lightly to restore shape in spring or summer
Privet	frequently when young to achieve basal thickness; later as required during summer; rejuvenate by hard cutting back in April

Prunus 'Cistena'	as above, but restrict new growth to 6 in. after flowering
Prunus 'Pissardii' (Blaze)	frequently when young to achieve basal thickness; when mature cut new growth well back to 18 in. after flowering in spring
Pyracantha	lightly, as flowers and fruit are carried on two-year-old wood; in spring after flowering
Quickthorn	frequently when young to achieve basal thickness; when mature trim to shape in summer
Rhododendron	as little as possible with shears to maintain outline; in summer
Rosemary	lightly to shape in spring
Rose	hybrid teas and floribundas hard when young; moderately to maintain shape when mature. Shrub roses need old wood cut out at base and long shoots shortened to maintain shape; main pruning March, shoot shortening in summer.
Santolina	lightly after flowering in spring
Sea Buckthorn	lightly in spring to maintain shape
Snowberry	lightly in spring with regard to autumn berries
Thuja	as for cupresses above
Yew	trim to maintain shape in late summer; rejuvenate at base by hard cutting back

14
The Craft
of Topiary

Topiary work harks back to days of gardening in the grand manner. Its natural accompaniment is statuary and terraces against the backdrop of a sumptuous building. If this were the entire picture, however, there would be little place for the craft today. But it was also practiced by the cottage gardener of old, and there is no reason why his present-day counterpart should not revive it given the freedom of style that is current.

Perhaps what we lack today is patience and the willingness to create a garden feature that may not reach full maturity in our own lifetime.

This is just a warning that topiary should not be attempted by the "instant gardener"—the one who is disappointed if something begun this year does not come to fulfilment next year.

Topiary in its pure form is the training of certain trees into unusual shapes by means of pruning with the use of such aids as ties and stiff wire. Two trees lend themselves well to this treatment—yew, which is ideal, and box. Both are evergreen, closely knit and with small leaves. Holly is capable of being shaped in detail, but with its larger leaves is rather less suitable.

Topiary shapes: a traditional interrupted cone

Topiary shapes: a free-standing
sphere

An archway of pyracantha.
This is strictly topiary work,
although a lot of people would
undertake it without realizing
that

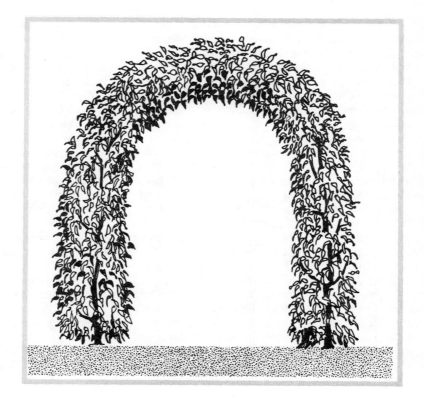

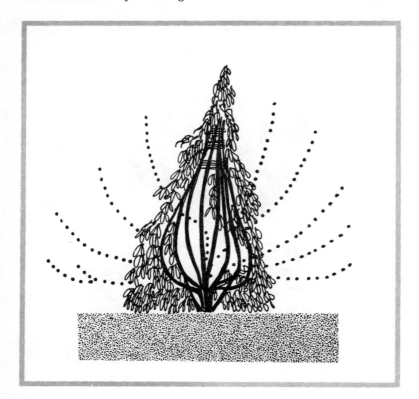

Four stages in the shaping of a peacock in topiary are shown here and on the next two pages. Note the use of wire or basketwork to achieve the desired shape in the third stage

A yew tree trained as a peacock can evoke extreme sentiments: some see it as vulgar and trivial; others find it the epitome of gardening skill. Less ambitious and perhaps more widely acceptable are geometric forms such as cones or spheres. Whatever the form, its creation is not difficult; patience and restraint are all that is demanded.

In all cases it is best to start with young stock from a nursery. A plant 1–2 ft. tall will in the course of a few years catch up with one twice as tall when planted, so there is no advantage in paying more for big plants. However, try to ensure that the young tree is well clothed with feathery sideshoots to ground level, as this will make easier the establishment of a thick base. It is worth repeating that yew is the ideal; box and holly are more loose and open in habit, making it more difficult to fix a detail of shape.

Topiary is like statuary, in that it is "built" on a stout pedestal or base. And one should also aim for a tapering upward shape, as with a hedge, because this allows an equal amount of light to fall on all parts of the tree with resulting even growth; it also lessens the risk of damage by snow.

So how long will it take before a piece of topiary takes shape? Yew should make a mature cone in less than 10 years; box or holly in half that time. To create a bird-form in all its detail it would be wise to double these periods.

Give the tree every chance of optimum growth by planting in deeply dug, well-drained and well-fed soil, and avoid exposed situations. The job of training really starts when the base of the tree rising from ground-level is considered strong enough in proportion to the proposed top. Clearly there must be some tipping of growth in the early years to promote thickness, but preserve at all costs two central leading shoots for future training. At a time which only the designer-gardener can judge ideal, these central shoots are bound together to form the connecting "stem" above which the design will take shape—assuming of course that the topiarist intends a multiple shape like a bird or a sphere on a cube. A tall cone—and this is a pleasing form—is developed from the very start.

The central tuft that is to make a second tier then needs to be divided so that growth may be trained in two or more directions. For

example, one part is directed to become a bird's neck and ultimately the head, while the other becomes the underside and tail. Every side shoot emerging from these "spinal" shoots should, with a little help, play a part in filling in the three-dimensional effect.

In the early years, shears are obviously the correct tool to use, but as the tree takes shape the long-handled shears or electric trimmer are called upon to impart the smooth finish. When to trim is largely dictated by the eye as the gardener will wish to maintain a near-perfect shape at all times.

It is not possible to persuade shoots to grow in an unnatural direction without the use of stiff wire. Fix this to the base of the tree if it is stout enough; if not then a cane or stake must be inserted alongside to secure the wire. Bend the wire in the shape of the desired design and tie convenient shoots to it with gardening twine. Ultimately the skeleton of wood will adopt the shape permanently and there will be enough leafy "body" to impart the detail and mask any faults. Remove supports as soon as the tree can do without them. Be content with a very rough outline at first; detail comes later.

SHRUBS IN BAS-RELIEF

For the faint-hearted who cannot face the long wait for the statuary of topiary trees, there is the alternative of enjoying a shrub carefully trained and trimmed to make a formal arch or symmetrical pattern, in bas-relief as it were, on a wall. The advice for pruning each particular shrub given elsewhere in this book should be followed, with the proviso that it is conducive to the shape intended.

Box and holly can be trained to clothe a wall, yew being less amenable to a single plant growth. In addition the following shrubs can be used: *Chaenomeles* (flowering quince or 'japonica'); *Cotoneaster horizontalis* or *lacteus*, *Pyracantha atalantioides*, *rogersiana* or 'Watereri'; evergreen euonymus, which is self-clinging; ivy, also self-clinging; and *Hydrangea petiolaris* which uses adhesive discs to climb. Apart from those mentioned as self-supporting, these shrubs will need to be tied at intervals to wires to keep them against a wall when they gain height.

In all cases the pattern of training is to select and lead shoots to maintain a pattern and to rigorously trim back others.

15
Old Trees

CAUTION AND CONSERVATION

It is not uncommon for a garden to contain old trees in need of some care and attention. Neglected fruit trees are all too common and the means of restoring them to better bearing are dealt with in the chapters devoted to the fruit. If such trees are in a semi-derelict state the most sensible course of action may be to fell them and replant with new bush trees that will be more fruitful and easier to manage. It is important, however, not to replant on exactly the same site.

In this chapter we are concerned more with the ornamental tree that is a garden feature and could not be replaced to the same effect within the lifetime of the gardener. It should be noted also that in some places a garden owner may not fell a large forest-type tree without the permission of the local authority, and that permission may only be granted if the tree is proved to be seriously diseased or to be a danger to property. A tree that obscures light may be cut back by the owner, or he may even be required to cut it back because someone else's light is obstructed. Restrictions on the removal of trees are wise in terms of preserving our landscape. Trees are part of our heritage, and it can be argued that we are merely custodians with a duty to preserve and enhance the landscape for future generations.

If pruning is understood broadly to mean cutting back and remedying faults in tree structure, there are several reasons why the gardener may need to apply these treatments. In doing so he enters the realm of arboriculture which is a highly professional field. This point is made because there are limits to what the amateur should do, and beyond them the expert should be called upon. Clearly the removal of large sections of a tall tree can be dangerous.

Full-time tree-surgeons are equipped with suitable gear and follow a safety code in their work.

But the amateur should be able to restrict growth by root pruning, to cleanly remove obstructive low branches and then protect the wound, and to fill a cavity in the fork of a tree. Bracing a weak cleft with a bolted bar or cable may also be within his capability.

ROOT PRUNING

Root pruning is a technique used to restrict the vigor of fruit trees and so encourage bearing, but it can also be applied to limit the growth of ornamental trees. It is best carried out over two winters, tackling one semi-circle of root area one year, the other the next. The point at which to expose the roots is below the furthest spread of the branches. At this point start to dig a semi-circular trench until thick roots are uncovered. These are the tap roots that need to be severed: do not remove fine feeding roots. As a rule of thumb, sever only those roots that are thicker than a broom handle—though tap roots of fruit trees may be thinner than this. Conifers produce masses of fibrous roots and some of these may be chopped out to control vigor.

TREE SURGERY

Branch removal must be thorough. If dead wood is being removed the cut must be made back into healthy tissue. Always cut a lateral branch flush with the main branch; this will usually mean first cutting away most of the branch and then removing the stub. Do not allow a cut surface to face upwards and so collect water, but slant it so that rain will be thrown off. If several amputations are necessary, spread the job over more than one year in order to ease the shock to the tree, and to

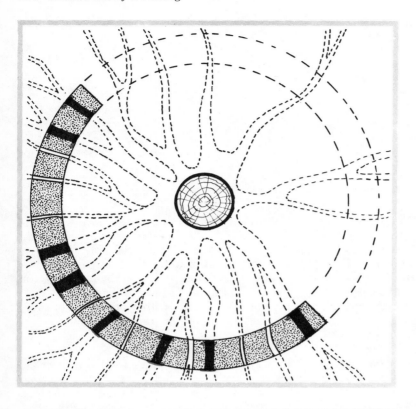

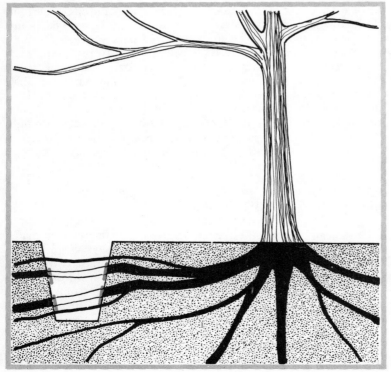

Root pruning showing above a
plan view from above and
below a sectional view through
the trench from the side

The removal of a heavy branch from old tree. A sequence of cuts is planned, with the last nearest the trunk, and the limb to be removed is securely tied to a stronger branch before the cut is made

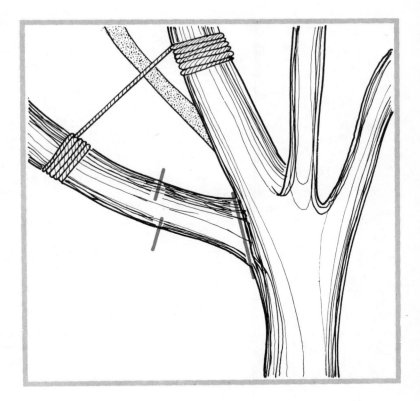

Removal of a large branch, showing how any stubby material should be pared away so that the cut is flush with the main stem

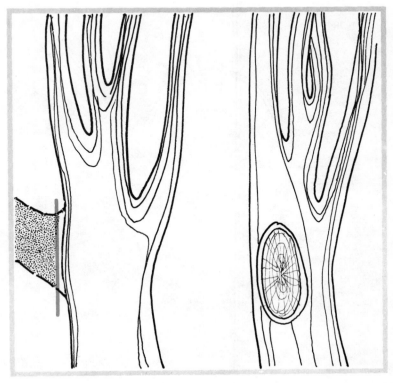

limit the production of weak water shoots that follows any hard pruning.

The safest time for most tree surgery is during the dormant season from October to March. Trees cut in active growth will bleed sap, especially beech, sycamore, maple and birch, and this prevents wound healing and invites the entry of disease. There are two exceptions to this rule on dormant pruning: *Prunus* species (cherries, for example) are pruned in May or June because of a specific disease risk, and walnut is cut in leaf because it bleeds less then.

To avoid tearing bark from the main trunk during branch removal, a heavy branch should first be undercut. Make the cut at least 12 in. from the final flush-cut to the extent of half the thickness of the limb. Then cut from the top slightly in front of the undercut. Support the branch with a rope slung over a higher stout limb before severing, so that it can be lowered to the ground. Remove the stub flush with the main trunk or primary branch.

Obviously a saw needs to be stout and sharp for this work, and a bow saw is generally the

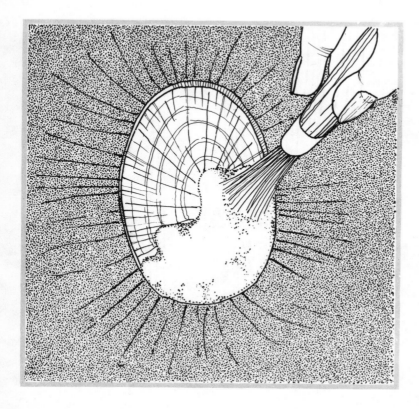

Applying a pruning compound to a large cut. The pruning compound acts as an artificial bark until the tree forms a callus over the wound

most manageable type. The flush-cut should be trimmed smooth with a sharp knife, any dead wood being cut out. A cleanly pared surface, especially at the edges, will permit the growth zone (cambium) just inside the bark to generate wound-healing tissue that will ultimately close the wound. To ensure healthy wound healing, however, all cuts should be covered with a wound dressing compound. Apply the compound as directed when the surface is dry. New tissue will form behind this antiseptic cover.

The same material is applied to a hollow or exposed cleft in a tree once the surfaces have been pared clean and dried. To fill in a large hollow in a trunk after wound dressing has been applied to the surfaces, use a stiff cement mix. Allow space for the repair tissue to grow and cover the cavity opening.

A split fork, fairly common in beech, may be bolted and braced. This entails drilling through both limbs, passing the bolts through plates on the outer surfaces and fixing a rod or cable between. Alternatively bridge grafting can be used.

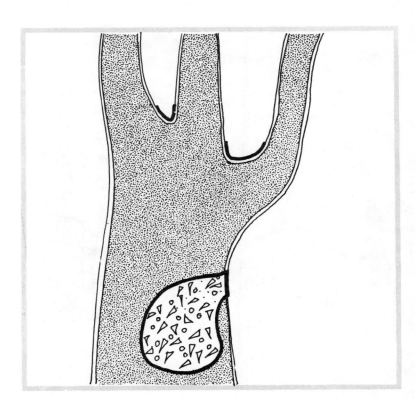

Cavity and cleft treatment in old trees. The cavity should be filled with a coarse concrete mixture and made flush with the bark of the tree

16 Greenhouse Pruning

Indoors or in the greenhouse there are a number of woody pot plants that can give an attractive annual display, but without a little pruning they tend to become leggy and fail to give consistently good results. These shrubs and their treatment are considered alphabetically below.

ABUTILON These shrubs have hanging flowers like lampshades. The commonest is *A. megapotamicum* with red and yellow flowers, and *A. striatum* with red-veined orange blooms. Prune after flowering by cutting back by half the previous year's growth from the main stem.

ACACIA DEALBATA *see* Mimosa.

ALLAMANDA Hardy outdoors in Florida and California. An evergreen climber with large, clear yellow trumpet blooms. When grown in a pot, pinch all shoots at about 9 in. long.

ARDISIA A shrubby evergreen with fragrant white flowers followed by hanging clusters of scarlet berries that often persist till the next season's flowers appear. Plants are at their best when 18–24 in. high. Older plants often become bare at the base of the stem and pruning consists of cutting these plants

Pruning of Allamanda. Caution should be exercised when pruning this plant as all parts of it, especially the sap, are extremely poisonous

Bouginvillea; showing where pruning cuts should be made

down to 3 in. above the pot in February when they should be dry at the roots and resting. When the cut has dried, watering is recommenced and two or three of the strongest and best placed shoots are kept, the others being removed by rubbing off.

ARISTOLOCHIA *see* Dutchman's pipe.

BELOPERONE GUTTATA *see* Shrimp plant.

BONSAI TREES Small-leafed trees kept miniature by growing them in a small amount of compost in a shallow container, and without artifical heat. Thick roots are trimmed back when plants are repotted. Shoots are pinched back during the growing season to get a balanced shape of tree.

BOTTLE BRUSH Callistemon An evergreen shrub with distinctive red flower spikes. No pruning is required, but straggly specimens need trimming to shape after flowering.

BOUGAINVILLEA A climber whose white

flowers are attached to colorful bracts and persist for a long time. Prune by removing all weak growths in February at the end of the plant's winter rest, and at the same time cut side shoots back to short stubs, close to the main stems.

CALLICARPA A shrub grown for its clusters of purple or lilac berries. Prune in February or March by cutting back fairly hard those shoots produced the previous year.

CALLISTEMON *see* Bottle brush.

CAMELLIA Sometimes grown as a greenhouse pot plant. No pruning is required, but trim out-of-place shoots in April.

CESTRUM Commonly used outdoors in the South and West. A rambling greenhouse-flowering shrub. Trim in February or March, shortening side shoots to about 6 in. and remove a few older shoots completely to thin out the plant.

CIGAR PLANT Cuphea So called because of the form of the scarlet flowers tipped black and white. Plants are not usually kept more than two years. In early winter one-year-old plants are cut back by half or more to encourage new shoots.

CITRUS *see* Orange, lemon etc.

CLIANTHUS *see* Parrots-bill.

CUPHEA *see* Cigar plant.

DUTCHMAN'S PIPE Aristolochia A climber with curious speckled flowers resembling a pipe. In winter side shoots are cut back to 2–3 in.

ERICA *see* Heaths.

EUCALYPTUS *see* Gum tree.

FATSHEDERA *see* Ivy tree.

FATSIA An evergreen with glossy hand-shaped leaves. No pruning required unless plants are straggly, when they can be cut back in spring. Does not need artificial heat.

FICUS *see* Rubber plant.

FUCHSIA A popular greenhouse plant with red pendulous bell-flowers. Prune when the plants resume growth in spring, trimming to shape and cutting out any thin or dead shoots. When growth becomes dense, cut back one or two older shoots.

GARDENIA Grown for its beautifully scented white flowers. With young plants, pinch out the growing tips during summer to encourage busy growth. On established plants cut back growths that have flowered by a half to two-thirds in February.

GREVILLEA ROBUSTA *see* Silk oak.

GUM TREE Eucalyptus Bears grey foliage the year round, with characteristic eucalyptus scent. Juvenile leaves tend to be rounded while later foliage is elongated. Pot plants are grown for the juvenile foliage. Growing shoots of young plants are pinched out to produce a busy head of the required size. When plants get too big, cut hard back in early spring to a few inches above the pot. Alternatively retain the branch frame-

The pruning of gardenia

Hibiscus rosa-sinensis showing where pruning cuts should be made

work and cut back side shoots close. Pruning every other year is adequate.

HEATHS Erica The various tender heaths (heather family) are grown as winter-flowering pot plants. Cut off the flower spikes when finished and lightly trim the plants to shape.

HEDERA *see* Ivy.

HIBISCUS When grown as pot plants they are evergreen shrubs with exotic wide trumpet flowers and a long central spike of stamens. Cut plants hard back in March or April to encourage new flowering wood.

HOYA *see* Wax flower.

HYDRANGEA A popular garden shrub easily pot-grown from cuttings. After flowering remove dead heads and weak stems. Pots are often stood outside during summer. Keep plants compact and prevent overcrowding by removing some of the oldest shoots each year during resting season.

IVY Hedera Decorative house-plant kinds need only trimming to shape. Over-large specimens can be cut hard back in spring.

IVY TREE × Fatshedera A cross between an ivy and a fatsia. No pruning required, but side shoots may be shortened in spring.

JERUSALEM CHERRY Solanum A popular pot plant grown for its scarlet berries which follow potato-like flowers. It is best to raise fresh plants from seed each year. To retain them for longer, trim back by one-third in March and then repot.

MIMOSA Acacia Hardy and cultivated in California. Has fern-like foliage and clusters of tiny fragrant yellow flowers. No pruning required unless plants get too big when they can be cut back by up to two-thirds after flowering.

MINIATURE ROSES Make excellent greenhouse or windowsill plants, but should be kept outside during winter and when out of flower. Prune in spring along with other

The parrots-bill or lobster claw, *Clianthus puniceus,* makes a rather straggly shrub if pruned where indicated

Oleander, *Nerium oleander,* needs to be pruned really hard to flower well. All parts of the plant are very poisonous, and particular care should be taken not to get the white milky sap in cuts or near the eyes

Poinsettia: *Euphorbia pulcherrima.* If these are cut hard back once the bracts have lost their color and kept fairly dry for a while it is possible to get them to produce another set of bracts the following season. In the wild they will make shrubs as much as 8 ft. tall so there is no reason why they should not do the same if treated carefully

The shrimp plant, *Justicia brandegeana,* also known as *Beloperone guttarta.* This plant flowers best when kept very bushy

roses, removing dead and weak wood back to a live bud and cutting old stems hard back to an outward-facing bud.

OLEANDER Nerium An evergreen with long narrow leaves and clusters of flowers at the ends of the branches in late summer. After flowering cut old flowered shoots back by half, and shorten side shoots to about 4 in. long.

ORANGE, LEMON etc. Citrus Easily raised from 'pips' and make shiny-leafed evergreen pot plants. Fragrant white flowers may be produced from time to time. No regular pruning required, but trimming to shape can be done in early spring.

PARROTS-BILL Clianthus An evergreen climber with scarlet claw-like flowers. Do not prune until plants get too big, when they can be cut back or thinned out after flowering.

PASSION FLOWER Passiflora A rampant evergreen climber with large exotic flowers followed by fruits which are frequently edible. Prune in February by removing the weakest shoots at ground-level or close to the main stem, in order to thin out the plant. Shorten side shoots by one-third if the plant is spreading too much; this may restrict current year's flowering.

PLUMBAGO AURICULATA An evergreen climber with pale blue flowers in summer and autumn. After flowering cut side shoots back to within a few inches of the main stem.

POINSETTIA Frequently seen at Christmas, and grown for their large scarlet bracts. When these have fallen, cut back stems to within 6 in. of the pot. Dust the cut ends with powdered charcoal to halt bleeding. About April or May shoots 3–4 in. long can be taken as cuttings to raise fresh plants.

POMEGRANATE Punica This plant, especially the dwarf form, is excellent in a pot and produces tubular scarlet flowers from June to September. The dwarf type

Grevillea robusta

Pruning of Streptosolen

Tibouchina urvilleana,
showing where pruning cuts
should be made

Hoya carnosa. Pruning should be done with extreme caution: the plant has a curious habit of elongating its new growths to its full extent before expanding its leaves

makes small red fruits from time to time. Little or no pruning is required, but in spring remove dead and weak shoots and lightly trim to maintain shape.

PUNICA *see* Pomegranate.

RUBBER PLANTS Ficus elastica 'decora'
Well known for its large shiny leaves. No pruning required. If the lower half becomes bare of leaves, do not remove the top as the plant will then form a bushy head. The remedy is to air-layer the plant and induce roots to form just below the lowest leaves. Make a slanting cut about halfway into the stem just below the lowest healthy leaf. Dust the cut surfaces with hormone rooting powder and push a little sphagnum moss into the cut. Take two good handfuls of moist moss and surround the cut, holding it in place with polyethylene film sealed completely with sticky tape around the stem. In a few weeks when roots are seen through the polyethylene, remove the covering, sever the new plant below the new roots and pot up.

SHRIMP PLANT Justicia brandegeana, also known as *Beloperone guttata.* Has clusters of pinkish-brown bracts. In February cut the main stems back lightly to maintain shape and encourage growth. Ungainly specimens can be cut back by half if necessary. Remove bracts on young plants until they have become bushy and sturdy. Pinch shoot tips to encourage bushiness.

SILK OAK Grevillea robusta An evergreen tree in Australia. Used in Britain while juvenile as a pot or summer bedding plant. It has delicate fern-like leaves. No pruning required. Cutting out the top of tall plants spoils the shape, and it is better to raise fresh plants from seed.

SOLANUM *see* Jerusalem cherry.

STEPHANOTIS A twining evergreen with scented waxy white flowers. Merely cut out weak growths in winter. When too large, main shoots can be cut back by up to half and side shoots back to 3–4 in.

STREPTOSOLEN Another evergreen climber, this time with hanging clusters of bright orange flowers from May to July. It is inclined to get leggy, so in November cut the older growths hard back close to the base.

TIBOUCHINA This lax-growing semi-evergreen shrub has pansy-like violet flowers from midsummer to late autumn. In late winter, just before it restarts active growth, cut the main shoots back by half and shorten side shoots to two pairs of leaves.

WAX FLOWER Hoya Bears white or pale pink wax-like flowers in hanging clusters from its climbing stems. No pruning is required other than the removal of growing tips once the plant has filled the available space.

Glossary

Apical bud Terminal bud of a shoot, usually of the leading or main shoot.

Balled roots A method by which evergreen trees and shrubs, conifers and some deciduous trees and shrubs are offered for sale. A portion of soil with the plant's root system is wrapped in burlap or polyethylene.

Basal shoots Those rising from near ground-level.

Biennial or alternate bearing A term used to denote fruit trees that bear heavily one year but scarcely at all in the next.

Big bud A pest which attacks black and red currants, causing the winter buds to become abnormally enlarged.

Bracts Leaf-like structures on a flower stem, which may be colored and so resemble petals.

Callus tissue Cells produced by a plant to seal a wound.

Cambium A layer of cells situated beneath the bark capable of being stimulated into division following wounding to form callus prior to rooting.

Canes Stems of biennial duration produced by most species of Rubus.

Conifer A group of woody plants, usually evergreens, that are in the main cone bearing.

Coral spot A disease which attacks both dead and living wood, having orange or coral-colored fructifications.

Cordon A single trunk which bears only fruit spurs.

Crown (of a tree) The framework of the branch system of a mature tree.

Cultivar Cultivated variety; one that has arisen under cultivation—often abbreviated to cv or the name is set off in single quotation marks.

Cutting back The removal of a considerable portion of the branches of a tree or shrub.

Dead-heading Removal of dead or fading flowers and the developing fruits.

Deciduous A term which describes those trees and shrubs which shed their leaves in the autumn.

Dehorning The removal of some old sound branches from within the framework of a tree.

150

Die-back	Death of a branch or part of a branch.
Dormancy period	A state of rest within a plant.
Double cordon	A cordon having two stems arising from a single trunk.
Espalier	A method of training, usually a fruit tree against a wall or support in which one or more pairs of opposite branches are trained horizontally; each tier of branches having only fruit spurs.
Evergreen	A plant which retains its leaves for a period of longer than twelve months.
Extension growth	Growth produced from a terminal bud.
Fan	A method of training a shrub or tree, either fruiting or ornamental, against a wall or support where all the branches radiate from a short central trunk.
Fastigiate	All branches growing vertically, parallel to the main trunk.
Feathering	Cutting back of side shoots along a young main stem or trunk to two or three buds.
Feathers	Short twigs coming naturally from a young main stem.
Feeding roots	Very fine roots on the outer perimeter of a root system that are capable of absorbing water and mineral nutrients in solution.
Fireblight	A disease which attacks many woody members of the rose family (rosaceae). In June or July dead shoots with dead blackened leaves attached can be seen, giving the appearance that branches have been burned.
Framework	The formation of branches in the crown of a tree.
Framework building	The training and building up of the crown of a tree.
Fruit bud	A bud which will produce a flower, as distinct from a growth bud, which produces another shoot.
Graft	The joining together of two different plants to form a single new individual, having the root system of one plant and the aerial part of another.
Growing point	A terminal bud.
Growth bud	A bud which will produce a shoot, as distinct from a fruit bud, which will produce a flower.
Half-standard	A tree having a clear stem of 4 ft. 6 in. on top of which the branching system develops; 3 ft. in roses.
Hard pruning	The removal of a large amount of wood from a tree or shrub.
Lateral	A side shoot.
Leader	A leading portion of a main branch.
Leg	A short clear length of main stem on a shrub before branching is allowed to take place.
Maiden	A single stem with some feathers of one season's growth resulting from a graft.
Oblique cordon	A cordon trained at an angle below the vertical usually between 60° and 45°.
Pinching out	Removal of young shoots with the fingers.

Pleaching	Training the framework of a tree to produce a screen or archway.
Pollarding	Cutting back the main branches of a tree close to where they arise from the trunk.
Pyramid	The method of training a fruit tree in which each tier of branches is composed of shorter branches than the tier below.
Renewal pruning	A type of pruning practiced on apples and pears in which there is a succession of shoots, fruit buds and branches and where the fruit is borne on laterals rather than spurs.
Replacement leader	The selection and training of a young shoot to form part of the framework so that an older leader can be removed.
Reversion	(a) A term used to denote a condition on a variegated plant where green shoots grow away at the expense of the variegated; (b) A term used to describe any tree that is changing back to the original species or variety from which the sport first arose.
Reversion (disease)	A virus disease of red and black currants.
Ripe wood	A branch or shoot that is thoroughly lignified.
Rod	A main stem of a grapevine and some allied ornamental species and genera.
Root bound	A condition which results from a plant being too long in a container so that the roots begin to coil round and round inside it.
Root pruning	The removal of a part of a root system of a fruit tree to induce fruiting.
Rootstock	The lower portion of a grafted plant.
Rubbing out	The removal of shoots as they first start growing by rubbing the hand along the branch or trunk.
Scion	The uppermost portion of a graft; the aerial part.
Shoots	Usually a reference to young annual growths before they have started to lignify.
Shrub	A woody plant that branches from near ground-level.
Side shoots	Young growth other than the leaders.
Silver leaf	A disease, caused by the fungus *Stereum purpureum*, attacking a wide range of trees and shrubs, but particularly members of the rose family (rosaceae), where the leaves take on a leaden or silvery appearance.
Species roses	A rose which occurs in the wild as distinct from one which has arisen in cultivation.
Sport	A plant propagated from, or a branch which develops on a tree or shrub differently from the rest in habit, size, shape, form or color of foliage, flower or fruit.
Spur	A restricted dwarf shoot system of fruit buds.
Spur bearing	A fruit tree which produces its fruit on spurs.

Standard	A tree having a clear stem of six feet on top of which the branch system arises; 4 ft. 6 in. for roses.
Stock	*see* Rootstock.
Stool-like	The habit of shrubs where young stems are produced annually at or from beneath ground-level.
Stopping	Removal of the growing tip to induce branching.
Stub	The portion of a branch remaining when a branch has been cut off but not flush with the trunk or the branch from which it arose.
Sub-laterals	Side shoots developing from a lateral.
Sucker	(a) A stem arising from the rootstock of a grafted plant; (b) A shoot emerging from damaged roots; (c) Shoots which emerge from below ground-level; (d) Young shoots developing along the trunk of some trees.
Tap root	Main root.
Terminal bud	The last growth bud produced in a growing season; the one at the end of a shoot.
Tiered habit	Where the branch system develops naturally from the same point annually, as in some conifers, or where pairs of branches are trained to develop from selected positions along the trunk as when training espaliers.
Tip bearers	Those varieties of apple tree which produce fruit buds on the tips of shoots instead of on spurs or laterals.
Tipping	The removal of the tips of shoots when winter pruning.
Topiary	Clipping of small trees or shrubs into ornamental or bizarre shapes.
Tree	A woody plant having a clear stem of 6 ft. before branching.
Triple cordon	A cordon in which there are three stems arising from low down on a single trunk, each clothed with fruit spurs.
Truss	A metal tie used for supporting a large branch on an old tree.
U cordon	*see* Double cordon.
Unripe wood	Shoots in which the process of hardening or maturing is not complete by autumn.
Wand	A one-year-old shoot of a willow tree.
Water shoots	Soft sappy growth which develops from a trunk or within the mature framework of a tree.
Whip	A single stem usually of one season's growth, either as a seedling or resulting from a grafted plant.

Index